AM I SANE YET?

AN INSIDER'S LOOK AT MENTAL ILLNESS

JOHN SCULLY

DUNDURN
TORONTO

Editor: Allison Hirst
Design: Courtney Horner
Printer: Webcom

Library and Archives Canada Cataloguing in Publication

Scully, John, 1941-
        Am I sane yet? : an insider's look at mental illness / John Scully.

Issued also in electronic format.
ISBN 978-1-4597-0786-3

        1. Scully, John, 1941-. 2. Depression, Mental. 3. Mental illness.
4. Depressed persons--Family relationships. 5. Mentally ill--Family
relationships. 6. Depressed persons--Biography. 7. Mentally ill--
Biography. 8. Journalists--Canada--Biography. I. Title.

RC464.S38A3 2013   616.890092   C2012-908613-4

1   2   3   4   5   17   16   15   14   13

We acknowledge the support of the **Canada Council for the Arts** and the **Ontario Arts Council** for our publishing program. We also acknowledge the financial support of the **Government of Canada** through the **Canada Book Fund** and **Livres Canada Books**, and the **Government of Ontario** through the **Ontario Book Publishing Tax Credit** and the **Ontario Media Development Corporation**.

Care has been taken to trace the ownership of copyright material used in this book. The author and the publisher welcome any information enabling them to rectify any references or credits in subsequent editions.

J. Kirk Howard, President

Printed and bound in Canada.

Visit us at
Dundurn.com
Definingcanada.ca
@dundurnpress
Facebook.com/dundurnpress

Dundurn	Gazelle Book Services Limited	Dundurn
3 Church Street, Suite 500	White Cross Mills	2250 Military Road
Toronto, Ontario, Canada	High Town, Lancaster, England	Tonawanda, NY
M5E 1M2	LA1 4XS	U.S.A. 14150

AM I SANE YET?

For my wife Toni, my son Jerome, my daughter
Emma, and all the patients and staff at the Centre for
Addiction and Mental Health in Toronto

CONTENTS

The identities of many patients, medical professionals, and others have been disguised to protect confidentiality agreements.

PROLOGUE

It seemed like as good a night as any to kill myself.

I was alone in my Toronto apartment staring at the television. I was lost. I hated myself. I was terrified of my new job. My kids were grown up, and my wife, Toni, was three hundred kilometres away. Why not do it? Why the fuck not? I burst into tears and shuffled to the cabinet where I kept all my medications.

I had a choice of more than a dozen different drugs to do the job. And there was the Cuban rum and Coke. It was the only concoction that gave me any relief from the depression and anxiety. I got a glass, ice, lime, rum, and cola. I drank it, then another. Then three more.

From the meds I chose the sleepers. I grabbed a bottle of the small, deadly blue pills. How many would it take? Thirty? Forty?

I drunkenly phoned Toni and said goodbye. She pleaded with me not to do it. I hung up.

The pills — *one, two, oh, fuck it, just pour out a handful. My god! I am really going to do it. Oh, god. I'm really going to do it.* I emptied most of the bottle into my left hand and gulped down the pills. I chased them with more rum. I was careful not to leave a mess for whoever found me; I screwed on the bottle cap and even wiped down the kitchen counter. I started to feel my death cocktail kicking in and half-crawled to the bed. I lay down, and without thinking of my heinous actions, passed out.

I had committed suicide.

Toni frantically called my daughter, Emma, in Toronto, and she called 911. The cops and paramedics arrived quickly, I'm told. But the landlord's policy stipulated they weren't allowed to break the door down. They had to find the superintendent to get the spare key.

When they finally got in, the commotion woke me up — sort of. I foggily remember seeing all the members of my family, except Toni, waiting outside the apartment door. They followed the ambulance as it whined its way to Toronto General Hospital. When I arrived, the medics gave me the standard liquid charcoal mix to drink so I would vomit up the poison. But I didn't puke. The fog, however, began to lift a bit more.

"Hey. Leila, did you see that? The guy didn't throw up!"

"I've never seen that before."

The nurse who attended me was a snooty, judgmental, suicide-hating bitch.

"Urinate in the bottle," she snapped.

"Nurse, I'm sorry but I can't pee."

"You can't pee. How would you like me to shove a catheter up your penis?"

I tried again, and this time streams of golden urine steamed and gurgled into the bottle. Ah, the odour of liquid suicide in the evening.

At seven o'clock the following morning the hospital psychiatrist came to speak with me. He was professional and non-judgmental, but in the end had nothing to offer me except counselling. I had been going to counselling for twenty-five years; if it had worked, I wouldn't have been there.

For most of that day, I was incapable of thinking straight or staying awake. I must have taken one hell of a lot of sleepers. I was undoubtedly immune to most of them by that time. That's why they didn't kill me.

John, after riots in Santiago and Vina del Mar, Chile, 1983.

Did I know they wouldn't? Was this a cry for help? No. It was way more than that. I had a flat, unemotional acceptance that I was going to kill myself. I had no self-arguments, no self-doubts. And I was pissed off that I hadn't been successful.

I have spent most of my working life as an international TV journalist. I started in television at the BBC. I was the youngest deputy newsroom boss anyone could remember. Oh, look at me! Then I crossed the Atlantic to work for the Canadian networks — Global, CBC, and CTV. I covered stories in more than seventy countries and worked in war zones more than thirty times. Usually I worked as what is called a field producer in the industry, so you might not know my face. Over the years, I trained and upgraded the skills of hundreds of journalists, camera operators, and writers.

So, what the hell happened? Why can't I think? Straight, crooked, anything would be better than the stunned, immobilizing negativity that has grounded one of the universe's great talents. What happened to the gift I had nurtured to an international status?

I've asked myself a million times, why have I, your journalist hero, spent a total of nearly six months in seven mental facilities and twenty-five years in the offices of psychologists and psychiatrists, my brain in aspic, jelly-like, quivering, wobbling from one lack of sanity to another?

Often I stare at walls — a hypnotic, unblinking stare that can grip me for as long as four hours, the suicidal boredom of a mind emptied of all emotion but sadness and despair — my only ally a white wall that hides me in a cape of desperate vacuity.

I am finally starting to learn how I came to be this way. And I think I'm getting better. The fact that I'm writing this book is probably the strongest evidence that I now have some grip on reality. But, of course, I don't really know if I do or not. As I begin writing, I am cranked up on drugs. I take up to twenty-five different pills every day. Some are supposed to slow me down so I can sleep; others are for different mental and physical wreckage. Anti-depressants do not give me a high of any kind. They are merely meant to even out my mood so I hurt less and function more. And, of course, I take one Aspirin every day. It's for my heart. That's a bit weird for a guy who tried to commit suicide, isn't it?

I've seen forty different psychologists and psychiatrists over the years. Yes, forty. This year alone, my visits to physical and mental professionals are up to one hundred. They say I am severely clinically depressed. No argument from me. I know now that I'm wired a bit differently from others. My genetics may have let me down. My upbringing in New Zealand may not have been the best, to put it mildly. My mom, my dad, my religion, my teachers, all may have contributed.

Or maybe it's just me.

This book is my story. The story of how I got to be the way I am. But it's more than that; it's also an attempt to look at mental illness itself. It's a book for anyone who has suffered from depression or has a relative or friend who has. It is for anyone who is aware that depression and suicide are on the rise and something should be done about it. I want to take you behind the walls of mental institutions and introduce you to real people with real problems. I want to examine their experiences as well as my own. I want to explore the world of psychology in terms of what has been working for them and for me in our attempt to escape from depression. And I want to answer the question in the title of the book: Am I sane yet?

1

CELL BLOCK ONE

You may ask, why should anyone listen to me about mental illness? Well, because I've been there.

Two days after my suicide attempt, I was placed in a cell-like prison. I would spend the next three weeks inside one of the closed male wards at Toronto's prestigious Centre for Addiction and Mental Health (CAMH, commonly pronounced *CAM-H*. It used to be known as the Clarke Institute).

In this ward at CAMH, you're locked behind glass and iron doors. The bedrooms have no hooks, nothing to hang your clothes on — nothing you could use to try to kill yourself. Even the bedside drawer was smoothed out and unable to cut flesh.

The washrooms and showers were relatively clean, but culturally disgusting, with no doors, no shielding of any kind; you sat and did your business out in the open, for everyone to watch and listen.

Embarrassment can hardly be good for the mind. I remember once I was trying to take a pee and one patient, a guy who was usually in an even more secure lockup, whipped out his semi-erect penis and began waving it in all directions. Yeah, he was delusional. The staff ordered him to park his penis and hustled him back to his own sealed-off world.

Despite the screamers, the ward wasn't dangerous, but it was grim and depressing. After I'd been there a few days, I was allowed to go for walks outside. Those breaks helped, but I always had to return to the cacophonous world of the shouters, the very sick, the sedated, the hyper-actives, and the hyper-talkers.

The care I received was, I guess, the best they could offer. Yet again my meds were changed several times, but I received no therapy. Although the hospital pharmacist dropped by to answer any questions I might have about my medications, I don't remember a word he said. I was too drugged up.

Slowly I healed, and after three weeks they decided to release me. The psychiatrists had determined that I suffered from depression, self-esteem issues, anxiety, and a bit of paranoia. Who doesn't? Well, unfortunately, mine is crippling. They also diagnosed me with post-traumatic stress disorder (PTSD). All those years as a journalist covering wars and riots year after year had taken their toll.

The following story will give you a hint of what I did for a living and may help you see how I and other folks get twisted up by trauma and shock.

The civil war in El Salvador was as obscene as civil wars get — eighty thousand dead, with bodies lying in the gutters and hidden in the bushes. Those scenes alone were enough to bend the brain and disgust the soul. In 1981, the CBC sent us to the village of Santa Ana, about half an hour outside the capital, San Salvador. Our crew consisted of a driver, a reporter, a cameraman, a soundman, and me, the boss. Unknown to us, there had been a firefight in Santa Ana overnight and a number of senior soldiers had switched sides. As bodies lay rotting in the streets, we negotiated our way to the post office to make a pre-arranged call to the president's office. Instantly we were surrounded by hostile, apoplectic landowners who yelled at us in English, accusing us of being CIA spies.

Suddenly, combat-ready police surrounded our van and ordered us to back up to the police station.

All the time the angry crowd was yelling "Kill them! Kill them!"

As we reached the police station, the cops ordered us out of the van and lined us up against a wall.

Oh, Jesus, this is it, I thought. *Execution.*

Reporter David flicked his eyes from side to side as if trying to communicate, but no words came out of his mouth. Driver Ruiz was shaking so hard he dropped his cigarette. He couldn't even beg for his life. Cameraman Bobby trembled; the veteran knew what was about to happen. Soundman Rick later said he thought about eating a Big Mac.

Me? I stared at the trees rustling in the warm tropical morning. *So this is death.* I thought. Curiously, I was not afraid. There were no thoughts of home, just "let's get it over with."

The police escort took aim. The crowd, who were going to lose a lot of their land to peasants, had the singular exhortation. "Kill them. Kill them," they shouted.

The AK-47s were aimed at our heads; fingers rested on triggers.

"What the fuck's going on here?"

A senior cop was just leaving the barracks for lunch. Another officer filled him in on the situation. He stared at us, then at the firing squad. Then he did something unusual. Not only did he want to inspect our gear to make sure we weren't carrying food or weapons to the rebels, but he wanted to read our research files. He picked out a *Time* magazine that was in one of the files. It contained a story about death squads, which could have had us shot instantly, but he seemed to miss that page. Instead, as he leafed through the magazine, he suddenly stopped and a big smile crossed his face. It seems he had discovered an ad for Miami tourism featuring a gorgeous, semi-clad woman. He turned to us and said, "Get the fuck out of here and never come back."

A bikini, the lifesaver? Ain't that a hoot?

On the way back to San Salvador, David did a piece to camera about the incident and we carried on with our day, including an interview with President Duarte. Back in the hotel we had a couple of beers and then dinner. Later, I began to feel queasy and decided go to bed. As the elevator doors closed, I pressed 3, then promptly erupted, vomit swamping the elevator. I couldn't stop.

It wasn't food poisoning.

There's actually a name for the condition one of my psychiatrists used to describe my state of mind, aside from depression. And that word is *counterphobia.*

Counterphobia is defined as the preference for fearful situations. It implies that counterphobic patients search out those things or situations that cause them apprehension (me and war zones?). While most phobic folks will take drastic measures to avoid frightening situations, a counterphobic will actively seek them out. This is assumed to be the individual's attempt to cope with some kind of internal anxiety.

Studies have concluded that people who have counterphobia have higher IQs, are fiercely independent, self-assured, and emotionally stable, but have an addiction to thrill-seeking. I love the bit that counterphobics have high IQs. Sure we do. Regular geniuses we are.

2

THE STATISTICS AND THE FALLOUT

Mental illness is everywhere. Wander through a mall on a bleak winter's week in the Northern Hemisphere — try the third week of January (some therapists nail it down to January 18). They claim this is the worst time of the year for sufferers of severe depression, obsessive-compulsive disorder (OCD), PTSD, and anxiety. By this time the Christmas presents have been put away in the closets, the bills are sticking out of the letter box, the dysfunctional family dinners have finally been forgotten, the New Year's resolutions have grimly defeated us, and the daylight is too short.

According to the World Health Organization (WHO), every year approximately one million people die from suicide. These suicides most commonly have their roots in prolonged depression. The global mortality rate from suicide is one death every forty seconds.

In the last forty-five years, depression and other illnesses have increased suicide rates by 60 percent worldwide. Suicide is one of the three leading causes of death among those aged fifteen to forty-four in some countries, and the second leading cause of death in the ten to twenty-four age group. These figures do not include unsuccessful suicide attempts, which are, as you might guess, estimated to be much higher.

According to data from WHO, countries in Eastern Europe, such as Belarus and Lithuania, and Asian nations including South Korea, China, Japan, and Sri Lanka, top the list of suicide rates.

And here's a stat that disgraces our entire health system here at home. A quarter of people hospitalized in Canada for depression were re-admitted to an emergency room within thirty days of being discharged. One study followed 13,000 depressed but discharged patients. It found nearly half of them didn't receive follow-up care of any kind. Five thousand descended back into severe, life-threatening depression. If I were you, I'd have a heart attack instead. An amazing 99 percent of heart patients had a follow-up visit with a doctor within thirty days of being discharged from hospital.

Major depression affects 10 to 25 percent of women — almost twice as many as men. Hormonal factors may contribute to the increased rate of depression in women, particularly during menstrual cycle changes, pregnancy, postpartum, after a miscarriage, or before or during menopause.

Men with depression typically have a higher rate of feeling irritable, angry, and discouraged, however, and this can make it harder to recognize. The rate of suicide in men is also four times that of women, though more women attempt it. Men often use violent methods to kill themselves. Women tend to take a more non-violent route.

Many people have the mistaken idea that it is normal for older adults to feel depressed. Seniors often don't want to discuss feeling hopeless, sad, a loss of interest in normally pleasurable activities, or prolonged grief after the loss of a spouse or other loved one. According to CAMH, depression is one of the most common mental health problems affecting seniors, yet it often goes undiagnosed and untreated. Because older adults are more sensitive to drug side effects (recent studies have also found that SSRIs such as Prozac can cause rapid bone loss and a higher risk for fractures and falls) and are often taking other medications that could increase the risk of interactions, antidepressants are not usually recommended. In many cases, therapy and/or healthy lifestyle changes, such as exercise, can be as effective as antidepressants in relieving depression in the elderly, but without the dangerous side effects.

At the other end of the age scale, depression in children is more common than you might think. Children are surprisingly susceptible to depression and suicide. Psychiatrists used to start looking for symptoms of depression in children at twelve years of age. Now they are seeing symptoms in toddlers as young as three. Teenage suicide, which is on the rise, has been well-documented in the media. Death rates among younger children are on the rise as well.

A child who is depressed may pretend to be sick, refuse to go to school, cling to a parent, or worry that Mom or Dad will die. Older children may sulk, get into trouble at school, be negative or grouchy, or feel misunderstood. Because normal behaviours vary from one childhood stage to another, children with mental health issues are very difficult to diagnose.

But failure to diagnose depression in kids can be deadly. In Pikangikum, a tiny, remote Native reserve in northern Canada, an astounding sixteen young people committed suicide between 2006 and 2008. The youngest was only ten, the oldest nineteen. Sadly, this statistic is not unusual.

Other types of depression include Seasonal Affective Disorder, or SAD, which is brought on by the weather and change of season, and can strike individuals who exhibit normal mental health the rest of the year. For classic winter-based SAD, light therapy is a common treatment.

Postpartum Depression affects women (and less frequently men) following the birth of a child. Estimates of its occurrence range from 3 percent to 20 percent of births, according to the Canadian Mental Health Association (CMHA). It can occur soon after giving birth or up to a year after, but usually occurs within the first three months after delivery.

The type of depression known as Dysthymia manifests itself as a chronically low mood with moderate symptoms of depression. It tends to run in families and is more prevalent in women. Some researchers believe this is because women may be more affected by the pressures of society and react more negatively to physical changes in their own bodies. Sufferers may experience symptoms such as low energy, low self-esteem, disruption of sleep patterns (either too much or too little), or trouble concentrating.

Researchers have figured out that there are several factors that may precipitate depression: genetic or family history of depression, imbalances in brain chemistry and the immune systems, or a major stress in the person's life. Symptoms may also be the result of another illness that shares the same characteristics, or a reaction to being diagnosed with another illness, such as cancer or a heart attack.

In some cases, depression may become so severe that a person loses touch with reality and experiences hallucinations (hearing voices or seeing people or objects that are not really there) or delusions (beliefs that have no basis in reality). They think everyone is plotting against them and feel intensely persecuted.

The most common treatment for depression is a combination of medications, education, psychotherapy, and electroconvulsive therapy (ECT). There are also some newer treatments available, but many are still in the trial stages.

It is a common misconception that people suffering from depression should just get over "the blues" and get on with their lives. Clinical depression is not just unhappiness, but a complex mood disorder. While it can suddenly go into remission, depression is not something a person can "get over" by themselves.

Clinical depression needs to be managed over a lifetime. Depression can often be managed and controlled by combining a healthy lifestyle with psychiatric care. Watching for early warnings of a relapse can help prevent a crash. But that's the tough one. No matter what preventative steps you take, it can creep up on you, then *wham!* you've crashed.

My life will never be normal again, but most people can and do return to function at the level they did before they became depressed.

So how do you know if you're depressed? The quiz below is a combination of standard questions that will give you some idea of what to look out for. I've done the test perhaps a half-dozen times. But I won't tell you what my scores were. That'd be too easy. When you take it, if you answer "every day" to a few or many of the questions, it does *not* necessarily mean you have depression. It could be something else entirely. Only a doctor can confirm your condition. But it's a good guide.

	Never	Several Days a Week	Every Day
Little interest or pleasure doing things			
Feeling down, depressed, or hopeless			
Trouble falling asleep			
Sleeping too much			
Poor appetite			
Feeling you are a failure			
Trouble concentrating on things			
Moving or speaking slowly			
Being fidgety or restless			
Thinking you would be better off dead			

There are warning signs that can indicate that a person is suffering from depression. The common symptoms listed below are only a guide, but a pretty good one, and many mental health facilities use these guidelines to assess patients. Many of these symptoms I've experienced personally. But keep in mind that there are also other symptoms that only your doctor can confirm.

The main symptom of depression is a sad, despairing mood that is present most days, lasts for more than two weeks and impairs the person's performance at work, school, or in social relationships. Other symptoms may include: a change in appetite or weight; sleep problems (a huge indicator for me); lack of interest in work, hobbies, people, or sex; withdrawal from family members or friends; feelings of uselessness, hopelessness, excessive guilt, pessimism, or low self-esteem; agitation or feeling slowed down; irritability; fatigue; trouble concentrating, remembering, or making decisions; crying easily, or feeling like crying but being unable to; thoughts of suicide (these must always be taken very seriously); a loss of touch with reality, hearing voices (hallucinations), or having strange ideas (delusions).

At the time of writing, I have not been in an institution for two years — and I don't plan to ever go back. But the shattering of lives from the pain of mental illness continues. In 2011, 17,500 Canadians were admitted to hospital after a suicide attempt. Approximately four thousand succeeded.

Suicide is perhaps the most "sinful" anti-morality play one can commit. It's nothing to be proud of. Well, hang on. Maybe it is. The courage it takes is phenomenal. It is a way out of the hurt that only finality can ameliorate.

Now let's get something straight: I believe it would be a wonderful world if no one committed suicide and no was one was depressed. And I believe that the impact suicide has on families and friends — the ones who are left behind to deal with the pain — is horrific. But the only way I can make any impact on this disease called depression is to outline the thoughts of someone who has been there.

I personally believe the decision whether or not to take my own life is mine and no one else's — not the state's, not even the family's — especially if catastrophic illness has made life unbearable.

So what makes suicide so heinous, aside from the impact on those who remain? Is it society's inability to accept that we do not know what will happen to us? Not knowing if there anything at all after death? If this is the case, why should we not take charge and take our morality into our own hands? I would argue that there are patients for whom suicide is a blessed release: the terminally mentally ill, the dying, the hopelessly bed-ridden. Why suffer? Why not make the ultimate decision to take one's own life or the life of another who is in pain? Is that murder, or suicide? Or is it the mercy of a good and nonjudgmental human being? In certain circumstances, I believe suicide and assisted-suicide are not only permissible, but necessary.

But this book is not about assisted suicide. It is about depression.

The M*A*S*H theme, "Suicide is Painless" is myopic nonsense. The dilemma faced by the torn, the ripped, the dying, the ghosts of today, is nothing more than an attempt to plunge into the greatest mysteries of them all: Who am I? Who will I be? Will I be anything at all? Or in the end will I be just a heap of ashes in an urn or flesh rotting in a box?

Now, I realize this is a dilemma faced by everyone. My point is that if you have depression, the question can be overwhelming and suicide can seem like the solution.

Let me tell you about Ian. Ian was severely bipolar, or what they used to call "manic depressive," but he kept it under control with medication. But at one point Ian stopped taking his meds and soon had an attack of a high — he went manic. He told his boss to shove it, got on a plane to London, England, and for two weeks, day and night, gambled, whored, and partied. He got into a fight, ended up totally broke, and was sent back to Canada.

Then he had a dream of world peace that was his secret alone and he convinced himself he had to go to the U.N. in New York to deliver it to the General Assembly. Fortunately, he had no money to get there. He calmed down in hospital and he and I got along well. Even at the daytime aftercare program, Ian still seemed to have been recovering.

But two weeks after I had last seen him at a meeting, a fellow-patient asked, "Hey, John, have you heard about Ian?"

Whenever someone in the mental health community uses that phrase, you come to know what the answer will inevitably be.

"He hanged himself yesterday," he told me.

Although I suffered when Ian died, for me and many others his death was a warning. My doctors, friends, and family have to head me off at the pass if they suspect I'm headed in Ian's direction. That means I have to be not only clear-minded, but also determined to live through my own potential corkscrew toward death, and to overcome it — which I have done, five times.

The battle to overcome depression was the theme of a short speech I gave at a memorial service for a man named James who killed himself recently. I had never met James face to face, but I had spoken with him on the phone.

James's friend Mike and I were work colleagues. Mike knew I was an amateur expert on depression and anxiety, and he was getting more and more worried about his friend James, whose mental health he felt was becoming worse.

Mike was making Herculean efforts to help James, but he recognized the danger signs: James was changing psychiatrists, changing medications, and becoming more irrational and psychotic. But at least he was still asking for help.

Mike asked me if I would mind speaking to James … maybe I could pick up on something and suggest a course of action that might help. I agreed, called James, and he and I talked for two hours. He was clearly a man in great pain, and in great need of immediate medical help. He was bipolar.

I suggested to James that if ever a place could help him it was CAMH. I suggested he go to the emergency department, where the doctors would take him in. The next morning, Mike came in to my office, beaming.

"You'll never guess what James did. He went to CAMH and they admitted him."

We were both immensely relieved. James would be okay. He'd get the best care in Canada.

Three days later, a dumbfounded Mike told me that James had been released from hospital, sent on his way. About a week later, James attempted suicide, but he still called 911. He was taken to St. Michael's Hospital, where they pumped him out and discharged him the same night.

Twenty-four hours later he waded into Lake Ontario and drowned.

I asked one of CAMH's top doctors why James had been released in the first place. Shouldn't he have been held in a secure ward and treated until he was well again? The doctor wouldn't talk about James's case, citing privacy, but he did tell me that many patients suffering from depression could put on a great act, and very often they fool the doctors into believing that they've made a quick recovery. The doctor also lamented the fact that mental health was at the bottom of everyone's list, when it came to both awareness and funding.

Today, CAMH is refusing to admit patients who five years ago would have been classified as very ill. Why is this happening? Well, there are simply not enough beds and not enough money. That's probably why they were so quick to release James. They needed his bed for someone "sicker."

Yet if James had had his skull crushed in a car accident, he would have been kept in intensive care, and then special care, and then he would have been sent to rehab. But James's brain was crushed on the inside. You couldn't see the damage. You couldn't see how critically ill he was.

This is what I said at James's memorial service:

> They tell us, sadly, James was not alone. Four thousand people a year commit suicide in Canada. That's eleven every day. Here's another startling figure from Statistics Canada: two million Canadians suffer from depression … 5 percent of the population.

I asked a doctor at CAMH what I, or anyone else, could have done about James's suicide, about the general indifference and ignorance toward mental illness. He was exasperated. Here's what he said: "We are at the bottom rung. Nobody cares about psychiatry. It's like we're still in the Middle Ages. All you can do is write and complain to the government — write to the politicians."

I did, and you can, too. Write to every person of influence you know. Work on the Amnesty International principle. Many letters will be ignored, but some do get through and action is taken.

There's something else we can do for James and for those living with mental illness ... many in embarrassed silence: Talk about it. Learn about it. Help get rid of the stigma. Use the word *suicide*. Use the word *depression*. You'll be stunned by the number of folks who'll admit that they or a loved one are suffering but don't know how to talk about it....

Read about suicide and mental illness. Learn about the drugs. Learn how some drug companies give psychiatric meds the shortest trials of all.... Be outraged by all of this. Learn. Write. Be an activist. And above all, talk. For James and all the other Jameses who so badly need our help.

I thought the speech was pretty good.

But it couldn't bring James back.

When people say they are thinking about suicide, or imply that they may be thinking about it, you may not be sure what to do: Should you take talk of suicide seriously? Could your intervention make things worse?

The famous Mayo Clinic says that taking action is always the best choice. The following list of steps was given to me by AIM (Alternate Inpatient Milieu), a treatment facility at CAMH, to help decipher the warning signs of suicidal patients.

The first step is to find out whether a person is in danger of acting on suicidal feelings. Surprisingly, most experts don't preach soft evasion. I was told to ask direct, tough questions, such as: Are you thinking about suicide? Are you thinking about dying? Are you thinking about hurting yourself? Have you thought about how you would do it? Do you know when you would do it? Do you have the means to do it? How are you coping with what's been happening in your life? Do you ever feel like just giving up?

Asking about suicidal thoughts or feelings won't push someone to commit suicide. In fact, it offers them a chance to talk about their feelings, and that alone may reduce the risk.

Even I can seldom tell when a friend I have met inside or outside an institution is considering suicide. But here are some common signs I look for:

- Talking about suicide, including making remarks such as "I wish I were dead," or "I wish I hadn't been born." (I feel like that when my depression is at its most severe)
- Getting things that could be used to commit suicide, such as obtaining a gun or stockpiling pills (I don't own a gun)
- Withdrawing from social contact and wanting to be left alone
- Dramatic mood swings, such as being emotionally high one day and deeply discouraged the next
- Being preoccupied with death, dying, or violence (this one floors me every time)
- Feeling trapped or hopeless about a situation
- Abusing alcohol or drugs (they distorted my judgment so much that I needed their permission to kill myself)
- Changing normal routine, including eating or sleeping patterns
- Doing risky or self-destructive things, such as using drugs or driving recklessly (this, unlike depression, is intentional)
- Giving away belongings or getting affairs in order
- Saying goodbye to people

If you suspect that someone you know is contemplating suicide, you should seek emergency help if necessary. If you believe a person is at risk of suicide, don't leave them alone. Call 911 right away or take them to the nearest hospital emergency room. Try to find out if they have used alcohol or drugs; they may have already taken an overdose. If possible, tell a family member or friend right away what's going on. Don't try to handle the situation alone. The most important step you can take is to get assistance from a trained professional as quickly as possible. The person may need to be hospitalized until the suicidal crisis has passed.

For more information on suicide and suicide prevention, please see the Resources section of this book for a list of websites that may be helpful.

The stigma of depression can make seeking help even more difficult for sufferers. People are afraid of depression. They hide it. They hide from it.

I didn't lose all my friends because of my depression, but I lost most of them. Not all at once, just a few at a time. It started when I admitted to people I was having mental issues, and it still hasn't stopped.

Stigma is a vicious enemy of people with depression and anxiety. It is a hateful ugliness that sweeps the world for anyone with a disability. Sure, depressed people aren't always fun to be with, but I ask myself, were those people afraid of me? Am I afraid of them? I have no idea how many of my friends suffer from mental illness in silence; sometimes it's too difficult to admit to the "awful crime" of depression.

One thing I remember about the time I spent in mental hospitals is that, outside of my family, only three people came to visit me while I was in seven different institutions. And it wasn't just me; this is typical in institutions everywhere. Unlike a regular hospital, there are very few flowers, cards, or gifts. People are afraid to enter those doors that lead into the world of the mentally ill.

And jobs? Forget it. Nobody wants to hire a guy who's bummed out, and word sure spreads quickly once they find out you're seeing a psychiatrist.

Outrageously, to make things worse, our "friend to the south" is now refusing depression sufferers entry into the United States. The terror-spooked, gun-toting border guards, under orders from their government, have refused entry to more than a dozen depressed Canadian travellers recently, according to patient advocates. How do the guards know? Well, apparently, police records are often filed after a visit to the home of a mentally ill person, and, according to Wikileaks, some of these records, which include details about the subject's mental state, seem to have made their way into the hands of authorities in the United States.

There was a case in 2010 in which a woman was refused entry because the authorities at the border had obtained a record of her attempted suicide in 2006. Clearly, the United States regards mental illness as a crime. Brad Benson, from the U.S. Department of Homeland Security, stated in an interview in 2011 that "mental illness is actually under our law as the reason you may not get admitted."

This could be one more reason the stigma of mental illness is so hard to eradicate.

3

A FRIEND INDEED

My psychiatrist was encouraging me recently to get in touch with old colleagues. "Talk about anything you like. It doesn't have to be anything heavy. Keep it light. Just shoot the breeze if you want," he told me.

So, heeding his advice, I made plans to meet and have lunch with a former colleague. I caught the right bus, got off at the right stop, but, because I was an hour early, I showed admirable concern for my physical health and decided to walk around Toronto's West End in the soaking heat for a while, despite the fact that it felt as if there was a chainsaw buzzing away in my lower back. (This mysterious pain had appeared suddenly several months previously — a combination of fibromyalgia and perhaps depression was as close as the doctors could get to a diagnosis. But the pain was fierce and debilitating.)

At noon, I finally sat down at the restaurant. My colleague had invited me to lunch to "pick my brains" about the Middle East. Funny, every time he contacted me, he wanted something, from editorial advice to my help with some seemingly insoluble dilemma. And I would find the solutions. Often, this took five or six hours, and in one case, a week. I was being used, and I knew it, but I enjoyed helping fellow scribblers. But you know what? There was also another reason I did it, so common in mentally ill folks: I didn't have the courage, confidence, or self-esteem to say no. In my depression, with nerve and judgment nowhere in sight, I did everything he asked.

But this time, the new, upbeat, take-no-shit me arrived at the restaurant unfazed and quite calm, if a teensy bit sweaty. The chainsaw in my back kicked into overdrive.

When my colleague arrived five minutes later, he oddly avoided any physical contact. I leaned forward, but there was no handshake, no back-slapping, and no man-hugs. No gesture of physical acknowledgement at all.

"Nice to see you, John," was all he said.

Odd.

As he slid into the booth, I remembered that my friend was fully aware of my mental history, my times in hospital, and so on. So I felt more relaxed. He had chosen an old Arabic restaurant. I had the hummus with pita bread. His kebabs looked fabulous.

To start the conversation, I asked him about his latest business venture. It was a though he hit a tape recorder in his brain, which he refused to, or couldn't, turn off. For a full half-hour I got a nonstop travelogue of the ancient ruins of Greece, stone by stone, Greek god by Greek god.

Won't he ever shut up? I thought. I figure that in the two hours we were at lunch, I spoke for a total of four or five minutes. But what a revealing few minutes they turned out to be.

At one point, he stopped talking about himself long enough to ask about my family.

"And, John, I hear you're writing another book," he said.

"Yeah. It's a book on depression from the patient's perspective. I use my anecdotes to show the really big picture," I replied.

Uninterrupted, I went on.

"It's all based on my lifelong illnesses, and I'm using my experience with depression to offer advice to other patients and folks who are afraid of the illness and the havoc and death it can cause. I'm old enough now not to give a shit what I say, so I'm writing this stuff uninhibited. Some of it's quite raw. For example, I write about my suicide attempt."

I guess he thought his training as a journalist could hide every emotion. *Show nothing*. He looked at me, unmoving, a human statue. But it was his eyes that gave him away. The eyes always do. They dilated for a tiny fraction a second; just long enough for me to recognize that he was shocked. I went on to explain that the book would provide advice and information about the therapies that had helped me.

So, what do you think your next question might be if you were my colleague? What would you ask any physically sick person, no matter how trivial or severe the problem? Yeah, probably something along the lines of "So how are you doing?" or "Can I get you anything?"

But there was none of that. What follows is my colleague's instant reaction as I got to the last phrase — *The therapies are working for me.*

He looked at me and said, "Did I tell you I've just bought a new Honda? Runs beautifully."

I felt as if my mental health had been dismissed the moment I mentioned it, thrown out with the garbage of life. He didn't want to (or couldn't) talk about it for reasons known only to him. Perhaps he suffered from depression himself, or maybe someone in his family committed suicide. I don't know. But I refused to excuse his behaviour, no matter the circumstance.

I had just experienced stigma face-to-face again, and I found it as egregiously offensive as any form of racism, which it is. It's discrimination, segregation without colour, mental apartheid.

I continued jabbing away at my hummus and pretending to be interested in the rest of his verbiage. He let me have another a couple of minutes to sum up the Middle East problem and then he was off again on some impenetrable tangent. We left the restaurant some time later, promising to make this a regular date.

Oh, yeah, like that'll happen, I thought.

When we parted, I made my way to the right bus, got on, and found a seat, but by the time the bus had chugged up the hill, I had begun to feel uneasy. I replayed the lunch over and over in my mind. I had noted his rudeness the moment it happened. Then, as the bus turned onto the main drag, I realized that my annoyance was turning full speed into rage and shock, which pissed me off big time. A day later I became even angrier as I developed mild depression; the shock of the event had triggered post-traumatic stress disorder (PTSD).

I began to feel almost irrationally, uncontrollably angry and fixated on the episode as the memory of it buzzed around in my brain in constant replay. It wouldn't stop — *twenty-four fucking hours later!* But I'm stronger now than I was in the past, so I fought it off. I thought my reaction might have been out of whack with reality. But was it? Stigma is all about fear, shame, silence, and the all-too-common mindset of "I couldn't give a shit about the mentally ill. I've got too much else to think about."

And my lunch colleague? "Separate cheques, please," he had told the waiter.

I didn't even get a free meal for my trouble.

"Everyone truly needs a pimp. And watch out for charmers."

The composer? One of the 1960s great punk/blues and folk singers, Mendelson Joe. He's a friend of mine.

Joe, who is just as creative as ever, is always interested in how I'm doing. He sends me CDs, postcards of his spectacular art, writes me letters, and calls me up.

After reading my first book, *Am I Dead Yet?*, he tracked me down. Oh, yes, by the way, this is my *second* published book. The first was about my experiences as a journalist on the road. It was critically acclaimed, but it didn't win me a Pulitzer. Anyway, Joe liked the book and contacted me. We hit it off right away and began to meet in Huntsville at the same Chinese restaurant for lunch every couple of weeks. Joe's stipulation — that we would always meet at opening time, 11:30 a.m., so the food would be deliciously lukewarm.

Joe always dressed like a cross between a paint-spattered Santa Claus and Cinderella. He's an activist, author, and constant public pain in the ass, a man of conscience, generosity, and decency. He would always eat two-thirds of a ton of broccoli with the piles of deep-fried crap. Me, I hate broccoli, so Joe did his supposed self-health trip on his own. I usually ate the gluey and sour chicken balls.

Joe was the first person I opened up to after I'd been in hospital after the suicide. He genuinely wanted to know how I was doing. And that's one classic way to help a person like me: Talk to me. Ask me questions. Just say hi. I'm not insane; off-balance, yes, but not threatening, dangerous, or aggressive. If you don't think you know what to say to me, you can try the most banal of subjects, like the weather. Why not? It always works. What would you ask someone who was physically sick? I just called to see how you're doing? Is there anything I can do to help? What's the doctor say? How are the medications? It should be no different for the mentally ill.

Joe can talk to me freely about my mental diseases, including the suicide attempt. I tend to hide nothing from Joe. Not all patients are as open, but they may be far sicker than I ever could be. *Huh? Who tried to kill himself?*

But here's the kicker: Joe paints portraits. And what type of person wouldn't want his or her portrait painted, you may ask? Well, me, that's who — I was reluctant, embarrassed, and self-conscious. But I finally agreed to sit for him, because it was Joe. I thought of entitling the painting "Mr. Platter Chatter," but I've already denied making that one up. Rats! (I'll explain later.)

But how's this for coincidence? It was fifty years before I sat for Joe that another portrait was painted, this one in Wellington, New Zealand. The subject? My father, Ben Scully, a mercurial man whom I will tell you more about later. That portrait was a full-size rendition of my dad dressed in his full regalia. As he grew older, he decided it was time to give it away to one of us four kids. The idea was to keep it in the family and keep his memory alive, or so I'm guessing. It was a classical, well-crafted giant; the only problem was that, growing up, we all had to look at it — a lot. It hung in the hallway at home, right by the telephone, so every time the phone rang, there was Ben.

We kids had a talk, my siblings and I, after Dad died.

"I don't want it."

"Well, I don't want the bloody thing."

"Nor me."

None of us could agree what to do with it, but we were each adamant it wasn't coming home with us. Perhaps if it had been smaller and less overbearing it might have been tempting, but…. Not a chance! Anyhow, I don't think anyone knows where the portrait ended up, so it's a moot point.

Portrait of John by artist and friend Mendelson Joe.

Joe has kept the portrait of me, hoping to sell it. I can't stop laughing at that!

But in all seriousness, I found Joe's understanding and empathy touching and deeply intelligent. He knew many of the theories of mental health and practised them every day. As I shed my disloyal friends, or they shed me when they found out about my illness, there was never a hint that Joe would lose contact.

Mendelson Joe is one of my guardians. And I have tried to be a guardian for others. Yes, I have taken care of other people over the years, the ones I met in institutions. Let me tell you about one of them. The next chapter is about one of the many people I got to know over the years who suffered from bipolar illness.

4

BILLY

Jimi Hendrix wrote a song about it — "Manic Depression." Today they call it bipolar disorder, or bipolar affective disorder. It's a cruel and often deadly condition. I am not bipolar myself, but I know a lot about it. My guess is that half of the patients I have met in the various institutions suffer from it.

The best way I can think of to give you my take on bipolar disorder is to tell you Billy's story.

I met Billy in a psychiatric unit in Toronto about ten years ago. He was flying. Then in his mid-fifties, the short, friendly guy had had a remarkable run earlier in his life as one of Toronto's busiest mechanics. That day he happened to be as high as Mount Everest; but the next day he could be weeping inconsolably.

He could no longer work and spent most of his days in or out of Toronto's Centre for Addiction and Mental Health (CAMH). He apparently couldn't get over the pain of a broken friendship from a decade earlier. For most of his life, Billy had relied on dubious electroshock treatments to ease his fluctuating moods.

When I met Billy, he had been undergoing electroconvulsive therapy (ECT) for an incredible fifteen years. More recently, a new therapy, magnetic TMS, had been added. Billy had refused to take any drugs for years.

It was ten to five in the ward on a cool March afternoon. A short, burly woman wearing a hairnet and hospital scrubs pushed in a huge aluminum food cart designed to keep the food hot (but it was always lukewarm). The fish they served tasted like the chicken, and no one could tell the cabbage from the tapioca. Each tray came with a patient's specially requested menu:

Appetizer:
Chicken soup, crackers

Main course:
Meat loaf, mashed potatoes, fresh garden salad,
assorted dressings

Dessert:
Custard topped with bananas??

It was unclear from the question marks if the cooks were unsure what they had concocted or if the computer took matters into its own hard drive and decided the entire meal was a mystery.

"I can't eat this shit," announced Billy as he tossed his food into the garbage.

"So what are you going to have for dinner, cornflakes?" inquired Laura, another inmate at the time.

"I dunno. But I can't eat that shit. Wait! Wait! I've got a cousin."

"Amazing, Billy. Have you had your meds today? Sounds as though you need them," proffered a helpful Jonathan. "We've all got cousins, Billy. How does that help?"

"No, no. You don't understand. My cousin is in the restaurant trade. Um, oh, shit, I can't remember his name. What the hell is it? Oh, right, it's Freddy. He said if ever I wanted some smoked salmon, just let him know."

"Smoked salmon? Your memory's not acting up again, is it? I mean, smoked salmon. You're not kidding, are you Billy?" piped up a usually heavily medicated Ayisha, who probably wondered whether she was hearing right or if the clozapine was just as useless as all the other schizophrenia drugs.

"Yeah, my cousin, what's his name? Freddy. Freddy. That's it! He can get me as much smoked salmon as I want."

"And it's free?" asked a suddenly interested Jonathan.

"No. No. Freddy's a businessman. But if we all chip in five bucks, that'll get us enough for a hell of a meal. Who's in?"

Frank stopped washing his orange and, like the rest, was intrigued by the offer. Was Billy off on one of his trips again? It didn't sound like it, and within minutes he had collected twenty bucks for Freddy's salmon. In the end it arrived — late and cold, but delectable, comparatively.

Another day, another incident at AIM, though this time not of the food variety. It happened one afternoon as some of us were participating in a group therapy session.

"Are we all here? Ayisha, Jonathan, Libby, Frank, Aleem, Marika, Eric. Colin? Is he here today?"

"He's not very well, so he's been sent back to Maui," replied Libby.

"So that leaves Billy. Anybody seen him?"

"He was on his way over. I think he stopped at the park bench for a cigarette with the alkies and druggies from Unit B."

"While we're waiting," interjected Jonathan, "I've been here for only a week, so can someone please explain how the Ontario Health Insurance Plan covers trips to Hawaii?"

"Hawaii? What are you talking about, Jonathan?" asked a baffled but patient Mae, the social worker who was the facilitator at that afternoon's group therapy session. She was used to strange questions from her patients, but this one really puzzled her. "OHIP doesn't cover trips to Hawaii, as much as we'd love it."

"Well, I don't get it," replied an even more puzzled Jonathan. "Libby just said that Colin had been sent back to Maui. And he's not the first patient I've heard of going to Hawaii."

"Oh." Mae swallowed, stifling a laugh. "It's not *that* Maui. Our MAUI stands for Mood Anxiety Inpatient Unit. It's in the old building. It's for more seriously ill patients. Some of you were in MAUI, weren't you?"

"Frank and I were," volunteered Ayisha.

"So was I," added the usually taciturn Aleem. Anger was Aleem's big problem. That's why he was persuaded to turn up for that day's session.

"Hey, everybody! Have you seen my card?" Billy almost ripped the door from its hinges as he burst in. Billy was on another one of his highs. "Here, take my card. It's my genuine business card."

He thrust one into every hand in the room.

"You're a doctor, Billy?" asked a puzzled Mae.

"I didn't know that, Billy," added Frank.

"Why do you think I'm a doctor? You think I'm a doctor, right. Oh, that's great. You think I'm a doctor. I love it."

"Well," said Libby, "your card reads William Hamilton, M.D."

"Yes, it does! M.D. — Manic Depressive!" howled a triumphant Billy. "Oh, fuck. It works every time. M.D., Manic Depressive. Oh, fuck, I love that one."

"Okay, Billy, that's very good. Now can we get started with today's session?" asked Mae.

"I got the cards made up at my brother's printing shop. M.D. Fuck that's great! Great! William Hamilton, M.D. Get it? Manic depressive! I get the cards free. I'm getting another one made up: William Hamilton, B.Sc. — Big Silly Clown. Big Silly Clown! Fuck, that's a great one."

Billy couldn't stop raving.

"Hey. I've just seen the address of our new fucking unit. It's number 85 White Squirrel Way. White Squirrel Way! Whoever dreamed that up must have been nuts! Get it? White Squirrel! Nuts! Oh, fuck, that's insane. Say, Mae, have you met my brother? Here's his picture."

"Billy, perhaps you could show us at the end of the session. We really should get started."

"Don't you want to see a picture of my brother? Here, look. That's him in the middle. Doesn't look a day over fifty, does he? Guess how old he is, Mae."

"Oh, Billy, I really don't know. Why don't you let me have a guess before the end of the session?"

"No, no. It'll only take a minute. Go on. Guess how old my brother is."

"Let's all have a look and we can guess, too," piped up Ayisha.

"No, I really think we should keep it until the end of our session. Tell you what, I'll cut the course short by five minutes, then we can all guess Billy's brother's age." Mae was a very good therapist who was trying not to lose control of a group of variously medicated, volatile psychiatric patients, and Billy's behaviour was not helping one bit.

Mae ploughed on. "So what makes us angry?"

"What makes us angry?" Billy was shouting now. But tears welling in his widening eyes had abruptly replaced the manic grin. "I'll tell you what makes me angry! You wouldn't let the rest of them look at the photo of my brother. Well, that's bullshit. Bullshit! You fucking bitch. It's a photo of my brother!"

Billy was screaming now as tears poured down his face and spilled onto the photo of his brother and friends yukking it up in a pub.

"Billy, Billy, I said we'd all look at it just as soon as we've finished the session. Now, please Billy, for the sake of the rest of the group, let's move on."

"No! This is bullshit! It was just a picture of my brother. You fucking cow! I'm not standing for any of your bullshit. Oh, Jesus, it's just a photo of my brother."

"Billy, I—"

"No! Fuck you, lady! I'm not staying here listening to your bullshit. I'm outta here!"

At that point, Billy lunged at the door, this time managing to rip it from one of its two hinges.

"Fuck! Fuck!" screamed Billy as he burst into the gloomy corridor dotted with rags that smelled and grunted and occasionally went outside for a smoke.

"Mae!" snapped Libby. "I really think you should have let us look at Billy's photo. It wouldn't have taken up any time and it wouldn't have hurt him so much. Poor guy is in a lot of pain."

Libby was not just furious with Mae, she was worried about Billy. She'd never seen him so sick.

"No, Libby. Only one person can run this session. I have to look after everybody's interests, and I can't let one patient dominate the session at the expense of everybody else."

"I think you're wrong. Anyhow, I'm going after him to make sure he's okay."

"If you do that, Libby, you'll be disrupting the session. Half the time's gone already. If you leave, I won't be able to allow you to come back in."

"Well, fuck you, too," hissed Libby, and she leapt from her chair and left.

"Well, we must move on," Mae continued. "I'll give you a handout in a minute, but first I want us to look at some unhealthy beliefs that may influence our anger." Mae deliberately tiptoed around what had just happened and resisted using it as an example of good and bad anger. She probably wasn't sure who would come off worse.

"So let's start with aggression. Aggression sometimes has short-term payoffs such as getting someone to do what you want through fear and intimidation. In the long term, you lose friends and loved ones and you can end up in jail. Learning to control your anger and be gently assertive can get you what you want without the negative consequences. Aleem, would you like to share your thoughts on that belief about aggression?"

"No."

"That's all right, then. Would anyone else like to share their thoughts?"

Frank wheeled his chair a little closer to the front of the room. "I would. I think that you showed anger and intimidation toward Libby. You were aggressive in banning her from coming back."

"Thank you for sharing that, Frank. Would anybody like to share their thoughts?"

Suddenly the door opened. It was Libby. "Well, Billy's okay," she announced. "He's calmed down now. I had a ciggy with him and he's gone up to Queen Street to buy a cup of coffee."

"I thought I said you would not be allowed back if you left, Libby."

"That was a joke, right?"

"No, it wasn't. It wasn't a joke at all. So you will please leave the room."

"Fuck, lady, it's not us with the anger problem. You should take one of your own courses. I'm gone. Gone right to whoever runs this place. I'm going to launch a formal complaint against you, Mae. This is not the last you have heard of me."

Milly Mart owner Abdullah had heard all Billy's gems a hundred times, but he laughed just the same.

"What are they doing to you, Mr. Billy?" he asked one day.

"You're looking at a first in North America!" Billy told him. "Fuck, I'm the first. Cigarette?"

"No, thank you. You're not supposed to smoke inside. But it's okay. I'll pretend I didn't see you."

"Fuck them. What a stupid fucking law, Abdullah. Can't even have a smoke with a friend. I'll wait until I go outside."

"It might be best, Mr. Billy. Have another cup of coffee. It's on me."

"Gee, thanks, I think I will. I've got those fucking magnets this afternoon."

"Magnets? The doctors? What do they do with magnets?"

"It's new. These fucking geniuses have come up with a new, totally useless therapy. I lie on a bed and they put these coils on my head. Then they turn on a machine and I get zapped with some fucking magnets or something. I dunno. It's all bullshit. I'm the first person in North America to be given the magnets along with the ECT."

"What is ECT?"

"Shock treatment."

"Oh. Do any of these treatments hurt?"

"Only my fucking memory. Jesus, it's frustrating. Sometimes I can't remember my house number. Or my old street name. My car plate number…. What? What were we talking about just now? Oh, fuck, fucking dementia. Jesus, it has to be like dementia, or Alzheimer's."

One of the more misleading depictions of the ECT (electrocardiogram therapy) Billy was receiving was in the 1975 Jack Nicholson movie *One Flew Over the Cuckoo's Nest*. More recently, CAMH has fired up its public relations machine and countered some admittedly distorted images with a fairly accurate and helpful up-to-date pamphlet and Web article dispelling allegedly erroneous beliefs. It explains the procedure thusly: "ECT involves administering a brief electrical pulse through the scalp to the surface of the brain. This produces an epileptic-type convulsion, lasting typically from fifteen seconds to two minutes."

But in Billy's case, desperate and frustrated doctors subjected him to almost unprecedented doses of electricity over the fifteen years. They didn't know the long-term effects of such repetitive treatment, but they did know that Billy was not getting any better. But he was not getting worse, even though his brain would eventually be zapped over seven hundred times. The magnets came after the years of ECT jolts. Billy was persuaded to be a guinea pig. Nobody had anything to lose.

Huh? thought Billy. *Nothing to lose? What the fuck! Might as well give it a shot.*

Billy did not really understand, or for that matter care what the magnets did to him. How bad could it be? He didn't even know the name for the new experimental procedure, one that had never been tried on an ECT patient.

A therapist gave Billy the TMS literature, but he couldn't be bothered to read it, brief and candid as it was: "Transcranial Magnetic Stimulation (TMS) … is a treatment involving magnetic pulses to the brain. TMS is being tested, but its effectiveness has not yet been proven although it is looking promising."

What the handout did not say is that although three thousand scientific papers on TMS have been published, none of them could or would say anything about the long-term effects on the patients, whose illnesses ranged from Billy's bipolar disease to Frank's obsessive-compulsive disorder to Laura's severe depression — although Billy was the only one sick enough in this group to warrant the risks of the largely unproven TMS.

Billy was already getting his brother to make up another business card: William Hamilton, TMS. TMS? Totally Manic Shit. Oh, Billy loved that one almost as much as Big Silly Clown: "I'll get my brother to make up one more card: William Hamilton: MD, B.Sc., TMS. *F-u-u-c-k*, that's funny."

Billy was one of the severest cases the doctors at CAMH had tried to treat. His entire life he had refused to take any drugs, so they had prescribed the ECT therapy. It was a long, long road he embarked on, but once a week he would lie down on a stretcher and have his brain fried.

Prospective ECT patients are shown a rose-tinted video that trumpets the harmless, wonderful benefits of the treatment. The video implies that ECT is grossly misunderstood and unfairly and inaccurately maligned. It's safe, they say, and has only fleeting side effects. In the video, patients walk into a warmly lit procedure room and are greeted by kind, smiling doctors, nurses, and aides.

CAMH is one of the world's leaders in treating mood disorders and it prides itself at being at the forefront of the treatment of most mental illness. But the institution is sensitive about its continued use of ECT, which is questioned by other hospitals and by many patients who have suffered severe or permanent memory loss. When Billy first started going for his treatment, ECT was still known as "shock therapy" and all that most of the rest of the world knew about it were the images of the crazy patients depicted in *Cuckoo's Nest*.

An information guide distributed by CAMH, and available online, states:

> During the treatment, a team of psychiatrist, anaesthetist, and one or more nurses are present. The patient is given an anaesthetic intravenously to put him or her to sleep briefly during the treatment. A muscle relaxant is also given to prevent physical injury, by lessening the intensity of muscle spasms that accompany a seizure. Oxygen is administered and heart rate and blood pressure are monitored. Although the anaesthetic lasts only a few minutes, patients feel groggy after an ECT treatment and may rest or sleep for about one hour.
>
> Usually the treatments are administered three times a week over three to four weeks, for a total of eight to twelve treatments. For longer-term maintenance treatment, they may be spread out, for example, once a month, and continued for as long as the patient and doctor feel is appropriate.

Possible side effects are said to include "some loss of recent memory or problems with concentration … (for example, patients may not recall what they had for supper the night before), but these symptoms improve quickly after the course of ECT is finished, over a few weeks. Some patients report mild memory problems persisting much longer after ECT, but this is likely due to their depression, not to the treatment."

I think that last one is just wishful thinking.

The pamphlet goes on to say:

> ECT is the most effective, and possibly the fastest-acting treatment for severe depression, and is particularly helpful for highly agitated or suicidal patients or those with psychotic or catatonic symptoms. Some patients receive ECT early in their episode of illness because of the urgency of their situation or their particular symptoms, while others may prefer to use ECT only after various medications have failed. ECT works well for severe mania as well.
>
> While ECT is highly effective at ending an episode of depression or mania, the benefits may not last more than a few weeks or months following treatment. Therefore, patients usually start or continue treatment with mood stabilizers and other medications following a course of ECT. Maintenance ECT can be used in cases where medications have not prevented recurrence of illness, or are intolerable due to side effects.

In Billy's case, desperate and frustrated doctors subjected him to almost unprecedented doses of ECT therapy. They had the fight of his life on their sanitized hands, but they had no idea if the treatment would even work or what the long-term effects of such repetitive treatment would be.

In the spring of 2009, Billy was released from CAMH, but he returned to the hospital often, sometimes for the ECT therapy, but also to see his friends. He used to call me and we'd talk, and on occasion we'd go for lunch or coffee.

So what kind of guy was Billy? Well, I once heard a nurse say that he was the nicest client she ever had. He wasn't mean or vindictive; just the opposite. He was generous, funny, smart ... and suffering.

His brother gave him money for rent each week for a tiny condo room in the downtown area, and Billy desperately wanted to work so that he could pay him back. At one point, a cousin of his gave him a job delivering flowers on weekends. But Billy loved to talk — too much, as it turned out, for the boss. After that he went to a firm that specializes in employing the mentally ill. I reckon they thought he was too sick to be helpful. They told him they couldn't give him a job at that time but that he should "come back in six months, maybe there'll be something then."

Billy was heartbroken. His seventy-year-old brother worked twelve hours a day just to pay Billy's bills. At least that's how Billy told it.

He then landed a part-time gig sitting in a car all night guarding a fleet of movie trucks. But it was the middle of winter. Billy didn't own a house heater, so he had to use up the gas in the car to keep the heater running, for which he was charged. He had no winter coat either. As it turned out, Billy didn't last long at the movies. A couple of gigs and that was it.

Billy was frantic.

How frantic?

"Could I speak to John Scully, please?"

"Speaking. Who is this?"

"John, you don't know me, but Billy has spoken of you often and I thought you should know. Billy jumped off the roof of his building this morning. We are calling the death in the paper accidental."

No, it wasn't! It was the terminal illness no one could cure. Poor Billy. He never had a chance. Life screwed him. And the doctors couldn't save him. I wasn't there when it happened, but I can imagine it. I've got a lot of sad memories of Billy as well as some lighter ones on which I can call.

Bipolar disease is normally treated with a combination of drugs and therapy, as I've said. Its symptoms are those wild fluctuations of mood coupled with amazingly rash acts when the patient is on a "high." Sufferers can stay awake for days on end during these highs, spend recklessly to the point of bankruptcy, and make grandiose, impossible plans. When up, nothing can stop the bipolar patient from believing he is omnipotent and has the solution to the world's problems — like that patient I knew who fully intended to fly to New York and address the U.N. Many patients say the "high" experience is wonderful and they don't want it to stop. Everything is so clear, they say.

For Billy, nothing was clear, except that he had to jump off that roof.

5

THE DIFFERENT FACES OF MENTAL ILLNESS

If there's one good thing I can report about depression, it is that it's an egalitarian employer. No one is immune — not the famous, the glamorous, the tawdry, or even the Icarus-nose-thumbers like me. And that applies to its ever-lurking cousins such as schizophrenia, OCD, PTSD, and other more arcane and complex forms of mental illness.

Post-traumatic stress disorder, or PTSD, affects men and women of all ages and occurs after an extremely traumatic experience. It is natural that most of us think about the condition in relation to our armed forces. For years, many of these men and women suffered in silence, but in recent years the issue has been brought out into the open, and counselling and treatment are more readily accessible for those affected.

But PTSD affects others, as well. The trauma can be triggered by events such as a near-death experience, serious physical injury, serious accident, violence, war, or torture — any event that causes extreme fear, shock, or an extreme sense of helplessness.

PTSD can develop in children, adults, and the elderly. If not recognized and treated, it can have serious repercussions. There are a vast number of PTSD symptoms. I suffer from most of them, but not all. Many symptoms are similar to those of certain mental ailments.

Some of the main symptoms include: an exaggerated startled response; memory loss; sleep problems and nightmares; flashbacks; trouble concentrating; extreme irritability; anger and violent abuse over petty issues; obsession; extreme nervousness and anxiety; muscle aches and pains for no apparent reason; unexplained fear; and low self-esteem or lack of confidence.

Flashbacks, when memories of a past traumatic incident won't stop replaying in the mind, are the best-known symptom of PTSD. Flashbacks can be induced by a variety of triggers, such as smell, sight, or sound. Once triggered, these memories are almost impossible to stop, because the incident seems real, with all the emotions involved. You may recall I had flashbacks after that awful lunch with my old colleague. It left me in shock and actually affected me for a week.

When a PTSD sufferer consciously or unconsciously tries to prevent remembering anything related to the traumatic experience, this is referred to as "avoidance." This may involve avoiding those close to you, or those you work with, which can lead to breakdowns in the sufferer's relationships with family and friends, or the loss of a career. So we have the perfect recipe for a form of depression, one that is very hard to treat.

PTSD can be managed if you find a good physician trained in dealing with the condition. There are some controversial new treatments that many swear by, but that I still have my doubts about. One involves taking the affected patient immediately back to the scene of the trauma and having them re-live it until it seems less horrific, even normal.

Oh, sure. As if I'm going to face another El Salvador firing squad.

I imagine most readers have had the experience of getting a song stuck in your head, where it stays with you all day and you can't get rid of it. Well, that may be how you can relate to obsessive-compulsive disorder (OCD).

OCD is something like that, only exaggerated to the point of mental illness. For me, one particular Richard Wagner chant used to drive itself deep into my brain: *"Weilala leia. Wallala leialala."* T.S. Eliot borrowed the lament for his epic poem *The Wasteland*. It didn't really matter what the words meant; all I could hear was the chant. I heard it at work, I heard it while I was walking down the street. That's when I first noticed my bizarre, infuriating obsessive thinking. Although I didn't know it at the time, this was one of the earlier warning signs of serious depression.

"Weialala leia, Wallala leialala."

At the time, it made me wonder if I was obsessive-compulsive. Apparently, I'm not, but I am obsessive, and it doesn't do me any good. News stories haunt me. I am attracted to them, but they cause me to have flashbacks. I am drawn to stories like this one: "Sixty babies are dying each day in one camp. Every 24 hours, more than 3,000 malnourished people arrive at camps already too crowded to accommodate them. The lives of half a million children are at imminent risk. And, in total, no fewer than 12 million people are fighting for their very survival."

These are the dry, statistical facts of life in the Horn of Africa. Behind them are uncountable numbers of human trials and tragedies: Somali children arriving at refugee camps so weak that they are dying within a day, despite receiving emergency care and food. This is already a humanitarian crisis of epic proportions — worse, much worse than the one that inspired Band Aid, says the director of a British medical aid agency in Kenya and Somalia. "We haven't seen anything like this for decades," she told *The Independent*. "Hardened aid workers are weeping at what they see."

The problem for me is that sometimes I weep, too. I am not even there and I weep for them. Stories like this one make me depressed. I can't just shut them out of my brain. Yet the experts tell me I am not obsessive-compulsive.

I have not been treated for obsessive-compulsive disorder, and I am not an expert on it, but here's what I do know.

There's a direct connection between depression and OCD, as studies have uncovered.

Obsessive-compulsive disorder is a mental abnormality that is characterized by intrusive thoughts that produce uneasiness, anxiety, apprehension, fear, and worry. These obsessions force the patient to commit aggressive, abnormal, or strange repetitive acts. The patient is unable to restrain himself. The most common compulsive acts include repetitive hand washing, extensive hoarding, preoccupation with sexual or aggressive impulses, aversion to odd numbers, and nervous habits, such as opening and closing the door several times when someone enters or leaves the room.

The disorder is caused by chemical and brain dysfunction. This doesn't mean that the patient has a damaged or severely abnormal brain, but some chemical messengers in the brain are involved, especially a chemical called serotonin. Serotonin acts as a neurotransmitter in the brain. Deficiency of this transmitter is linked to OCD. There is a movement that posits serotonin plays no part in mental illness. Science has proven them completely wrong, but still they persist.

Genetics also play a part, and 30 percent of Americans with OCD have a family history of the illness.

Schizophrenia affects about 1 percent of Canadians. In most cases, symptoms appear in young adulthood, but early diagnosis and appropriate treatment and support can help to minimize the impact of this potentially debilitating illness. According to a 1999 study, approximately 40 to 60 percent of individuals with schizophrenia attempt suicide, and they are between 15 to 25 times more likely than the general population to die from a suicide attempt.

So, yeah, mental illness is, if you'll forgive the expression, maddeningly imprecise, unfathomable, and deeply perplexing. It affects people from all walks of life and can strike at any age and in multiple levels of severity.

6

DEPRESSION AND ADDICTION

I do fancy myself an expert on addiction, and booze, too. I am perfect for the job. I guess the question is: What substance didn't I abuse? Way back as a five-year-old boy, I was already addicted to the asthma drugs. It was just a short skip to booze. In New Zealand, it was one's rite of passage to get hammered every Saturday afternoon and puke your guts out while still a year under the eighteen-year age limit.

There have been lots of periods in my life when I drank too much. I don't drink too much now. In fact, I am even able to have the odd beer, but millions of us can't do that.

The World Health Organization reports that approximately 2.5 million people die each year from alcohol-related causes. Here's a breakdown of the statistics:

- 5 percent of deaths from diseases of the circulatory system

[are a direct cause of alcohol abuse]
- 15 percent of deaths from diseases of the respiratory system
- 30 percent of deaths from fires
- 30 percent of drowning deaths
- 30 percent of suicides
- 40 percent of deaths due to accidental falls
- 45 percent of deaths due to automobile accidents
- 60 percent of homicides

The first mention of depression and addiction in human history seems to have been farther back than first thought. Early man and woman may have been bitten by depression and desperately searched for relief. According to CMHA, references to postpartum depression date back as far as the 4th century BC. The discovery of beer jugs from the late Stone Age period suggests that fermented beverages could have been ingested by humans since around 10000 BC.

The following are two incidents involving alcohol that I witnessed during my travels in Russia some years ago.

The first occurred when I was in Moscow one drizzly afternoon around 4:00 p.m. and, on my way down to the subway station, I caught a glimpse of something out of the corner of my eye. When I took a closer look, I realized it was a man lying on the sidewalk, dead. Apparently, this scene was so commonplace in the city that passersby were just stepping around the poor booze-addicted wretch.

Another day, I was driving along when I spotted two men so drunk that they couldn't walk, but they couldn't seem to fall either. They'd hooked arms, driven out of their minds by massive quantities of cheap vodka, no doubt. They half-lurched and half-ran from one edge of the sidewalk to the other, bounced off a fence back across the sidewalk and smashed hard into a phone box. When I looked back I saw blood, glass, and two heaps lying on the ground. I was advised not to stop, as I would make an easy target for the police.

The drunks were everywhere. The former Soviet Union has a well-deserved reputation for binge drinking, alcoholism, and alcohol-related deaths. What is it in the national psyche that compels these people to drink their lives away? Many addictions can be traced back to depression. A gloomier, more brutalized people are hard to find. A long history of hardship, repression, and ghastly abuses of human rights by the secret police has left many in the country depressed, beaten, and afraid. Vodka is their path to grand Russian salvation, or, more accurately, their ultimate psychiatric drug. But it kills them.

In many poor countries, I've seen the people make hooch out of whatever they can find in their fetid, disease-swamped shanties — filthy water, maybe some cleaning fluid — whatever gives them a brain-rotting buzz. And they drink a lot of this stuff. Very cheap, very bad beer is also available, and drunkenness is common on the streets in many places. Some Western tourists scoff at these primitive habits and behaviours, especially when they see these drunken locals. *Bloody peasants. Can't they learn manners, at least?*

This skewed perspective is illustrated by an incident that I observed during one of my trips to El Salvador. It was 5:00 p.m. on a weekday, and the brutal heat choked the men sitting around the cantina having an after-work beer. One of the men had drunk too much and had draped himself around a telegraph pole, to which he hung on tightly.

A Westerner who witnessed this commented, "Look at that lazy, drunken idiot. They're all the same down here. No idea how to behave."

A Latino man nearby replied: "Ah, but sir, you would drink too if you had to work in the scorching fields all day for almost nothing. This poor man works so hard because his needs are desperate and he's little money for his family. So he drinks to ease his pain. Beer is about all he can buy from his terrible work — cane-cutting. He works and drinks to survive. You Westerners work to buy things reserved for the rich white man. We work, we try to survive. You live and try to feel even better. You have a personality that twists and winds through moral right and wrong, good and bad, help and destruction. And with it comes your excesses. You demand a right to what you *want*, not what you *need*."

But there are some astonishing statistics that cast a black pall over many of our own young folks in North America. Boys who drink booze and binge-drink are nearly three times as likely to suffer from depression; and those who've abused drugs are six times more likely to have symptoms of the disease. Girls who drink alcohol are an astounding eighteen times more likely to suffer from depression than girls who abstain. But regardless, booze is the big hit with most young people.

According to a CAMH study released in 2011, the number of daily drinkers increased substantially in Ontario between 2002 and 2009. Marijuana use is also on the rise, and it's also becoming more common for users to mix the two. The most common regular users of both — those who haven't graduated from high school — also have a higher probability of mental illness. Some scientists believe that this suggests economic well-being, or lack of it, can play a direct role, not only in physical health, but in mental health too. Dr. Robert Mann of CAMH states that "These increases are concerning, as cannabis may increase the risk of psychosis for people who are predisposed to schizophrenia, and it may worsen the symptoms of other mental disorders."

If you are suffering from the pain of addiction, there is help out there. CAMH and organizations such as Alcoholics Anonymous (AA) and Narcotics Anonymous (NA) provide support. In this modern world, nutrition and metabolic care clinics can also be a beneficial part of the healing process. But the devastation of alcoholism and addiction is as hard to cure as fierce depression, and often the two go hand in hand. No addictive drugs should ever be taken lightly, especially when the user is already suffering from a mental illness. They can be wicked killers when misused.

Just saying no isn't going to achieve much. We have to get to the core of the problem, as always. The answers may be buried deep in one's "soul" and take years to find. But if you don't take that initial step on the road to recovery, it won't happen.

7

IT CAN HAPPEN TO ANYONE

It's obvious; depression crosses all classes, striking the talented, the rich, the famous, and the accomplished, as well as us ordinary folks. Anyone is a potential sufferer. The list of famous people with depression seems to never end.

Van Gogh, the artist, was a sad, depressed, ear-lopping genius. But that was in the olden days. More recently, in the 1980s, broadcaster Mike Wallace was diagnosed with clinical depression, but at the time he kept his illness a secret, afraid of the repercussions. Several years later, he finally revealed his condition in a televised interview and admitted that he had even attempted suicide.

Samuel Beckett is no surprise if you have read his bizarre play *Waiting for Godot*. Even Sting, the idol of the pop world, was in depression agony for two years. And Terry Bradshaw, the North American football god, was a sufferer; oddly, he had panic attacks *after* the games.

Famous people who have been stricken with bipolar disease (manic depression) include Margot Kidder, the Canadian actress and *Superman* star who turned up in a stranger's yard, filthy and broken, in 1996; Margaret Trudeau, wife of Prime Minister Pierre; Ben Stiller, the American comic actor; Sinead O'Connor, Ireland's rebellious singer, who attempted suicide twice; Beethoven (man, was he messed up); songstress Rosemary Clooney; Beach Boy Brian Wilson; and Sylvia Plath, the maudlin poet who killed herself when she was only thirty.

More recently, talented pop and jazz singer Amy Winehouse drank herself to death in her London apartment on June 23, 2011. She had admitted in several interviews that she suffered from manic depression.

Graham Greene, the great English author, whose life has been described as one of gross decadence and hypocrisy, "proving yet again that geniuses are often the most amoral of men," also suffered from the disorder. Way to go, Graham. Brighton rocks!

"The most amoral of men." It' a riveting statement, but also a classic misjudgment that shows a lack of understanding of bipolar disease at the time. Sure, many articles portray Greene as an incurable philanderer and a nasty human being. It's said that after leaving his pregnant wife and two kids, he had wild, non-stop sex with hundreds of prostitutes. He was also an alcoholic.

Anyone with rudimentary knowledge of mental illness would have known what was wrong with Greene. Like many of us, his actions screamed that he was ill. Greene knew he had bipolar disease, but doesn't seem to have done much about it, except complain how it affected his writing and his view of life. Guess how old he was when he died: eighty-six. Even so, please don't follow Greene's fluke example unless it's to write another *Power and the Glory*.

Many famous athletes have unwittingly been playing in games that have affected their mental health for decades. They didn't know any better. Only recently has this danger been widely acknowledged. Hockey has been in the spotlight lately, but the "head games" apply to football, soccer, rugby, boxing — all contact sports. In the worst scenarios, the result can be severe depression, which in turn can lead to suicide. One of the most stunning examples occurred in 2007 when professional wrestler Chris

Benoit killed his wife, his son, and then himself over a three-day period. An autopsy later showed that Benoit's brain was "so severely damaged it resembled the brain of an 85-year-old Alzheimer's patient."

There have been official consultations with industry bosses that acknowledge concussions and brain injuries sustained while playing these sports have been hidden in the past.

The biggest danger area is the number of concussions that go undiagnosed, leading to potentially more debilitating and even fatal second-impact injuries. Some researchers say that in football and hockey the number of actual concussions is six or seven times higher than the number diagnosed. Those numbers in hockey stem from research done in Canada in which physicians watched and counted the number of likely concussions in a game.

And then there's the over-the-hill mob. Their playing days are often years behind them when their head starts to hurt. Research in Canada with cadaver brains found the brains of many former football and hockey players are mashed up like porridge. Researchers were stunned at the damage, and the number of suicides.

According to the Centers for Disease Control and Prevention (CDC), emergency room visits by children and adolescents for brain injuries recently jumped more than 60 percent in just eight years — an increase from 150,000 visits in 2001 to 250,000 in 2009. Most visits among those nineteen years of age and younger were because of traumatic brain injuries sustained during participation in recreational activities. According to the study, the sports most likely to lead to head injuries are cycling, football, playground activities, basketball, and soccer.

"We believe that one reason for the increase in emergency department visits among children and adolescents may be a result of the growing awareness among parents and coaches about the need for individuals with a suspected brain injury to be seen by a health care professional," said Dr. Linda C. Degutis, director of CDC's National Center for Injury Prevention and Control.

The CDC is now fighting against brain injuries with its Heads Up initiative. The program has produced a very good fact sheet dedicated to educating parents about the dangers of concussions. It warns that even if an injury does not appear to be serious, it can have lasting repercussions if left untreated, affecting memory, behaviour, learning, and emotional development.

8
MY STORY: THE EARLY YEARS

Although I did take some whacks on the rugby field, as far as I know my depression was not caused by a concussion. You can be the judge of what did cause it as I take you through my life to hopefully provide some insight into the mental illnesses I suffer from.

The doctors started giving me serious meds when I was two. I would stare into the blackness of night, gasping and wondering if this time I was going to die. Crippling asthma introduced me to needles of adrenaline and bottles of happy pills called ephedrine, which left me floating through a translucent world where sanity was a passing whim. And there was also the eczema, onto which my mom slathered stinking khaki cream twenty-four hours a day. The skin condition persisted throughout my teenage years and into adulthood.

So, there was asthma, doctors, needles, worry, and anxiety. And to make things worse, just as I turned six, I was fitted with new dorky wire

John and his sister Jeanette, Westport, New Zealand, 1945.

spectacles. Gosh. That's why I hadn't been able to see a thing on the rugby field: "Oh, Scully, go after the ball, for heaven's sake! It's right beside you," Father Coach would yell.

When my eldest sister saw me in my new glasses, she added to her list of nicknames for me "gig lamps." Sister Jeanette claims no recollection of the name-calling, but she says I stabbed her in the leg around that time and she still has the scar fifty years later. Kids!

At home, the punishment for us kids "playing up" was frequent hits with Dad's razor strap ... the strip of leather on which men sharpened their cut-throat razors. I think my parents and others would be jailed for child abuse if they used such discipline today. But that's the way it was back then. One of my sisters implied that I didn't get belted nearly as much as them because I was my parents' pet. That may well have been true, but if so, I was one very sick pet.

Before I continue, let me tell you a bit about my father. Gardening and golf were my dad's hobbies (and duck shooting, and boxing, and wrestling, and horseracing). He was on all the right committees, with the shakers and movers, and saw himself as an important man about town. During my childhood he was a judge in New Zealand, and I, like everyone else around Wellington, respected him.

When he retired and became Chief Justice of Western Samoa, my dad wanted to give me his prized 12-guage shotgun. But I couldn't accept it. Yeah, the gun thing; I had hated them since I was a kid, and over the years I have sadly seen first-hand the death and destruction they've caused around the world.

My dad, who worried about me almost as much as my mom did, was an enigma. For example, when I was around age six, my parents were so desperate about my health that they tried several bizarre "cures": They flew me around in an open Tiger Moth biplane for half an hour. Cliffy, the neighbourhood butcher, swore that running around a chopping block would banish the asthma. And Dad even put me on his shoulders and carried me up and down the beach in the hope that the sea air would ease my condition. (It didn't.)

My dad would stop at nothing if he thought something would help me to get better. He was complex, yet simplistic, and he craved attention, probably because he never got any himself as a kid.

Portrait of John's father, "Ben" Scully, Chief Justice of Western Samoa.

My mom was born in Southland, New Zealand, into penury, and was more deprived of attention than my father was. Her mother was too poor to keep her. In a heartbreaking death-bed letter, my mom's mother poured out her despair and sadness at the prospect of losing her daughter. What does that do to a kid? To the mother? Depression anyone? Bog-thick Roman Catholic relatives literally snatched Mom and a bunch of the other kids away from the family home so they could preserve the Catholic religion in each of them.

My mom moved to Westport when she was a young woman and got a job as a stenographer at the local daily rag, *The Westport News*. Rag? Surely, I jest (surely, I don't). She then married my dad, and we four kids were born in quick succession; I was the only sick one. For much of my childhood, I would wake up in the middle of the night, gasping. I'd call out "Mom. Puffer!" And almost every night, for an hour, my mom's sleep was ruined as she filled an inhaler, or puffer, with a liquid called aspaxadrine and pump, pump, pumped it into my lungs. If that didn't work, she'd call the doctor.

When I was just a boy, a teacher labelled me "stupid" and my parents accepted the decision. I certainly was ignorant, having missed much of every school year because of the asthma. To make things worse, when I *was* in class, I was usually zonked on meds.

This was the start of it all.

Mom made all us kids go to the Roman Catholic ritual of confession every week. I remember once, when I was seven, bursting to have a pee but having to wait my turn to confess my dreadful, murderous sins to the priest. There were two sinners ahead of me, kneeling in the pews at St. Canice's Church, hoping the priest didn't give them an entire rosary for penance.

Oh, God, hurry up. I can't hold on much longer, I remember thinking.

When it was my turn, I got halfway through my list of sinful deeds, such as saying the word *damn*, when my own dam broke. The confessional was flooded with pee and my shorts were soaked. I splashed out of there and ran like hell. I hid behind the rugby stadium for an hour until I thought I was dry enough to go home and no one would notice.

"John. What's that on your shorts?"

"Oh, uh, I spilled some water on them, Mom."

"Well, you'd better change them and have a shower."

"Yes, Mom."

My childhood wasn't all doom and gloom, however, and I did have some fun when I was a kid. When I was six, the circus came to town, and when three rather old and very wrinkled elephants were led up the main street, dropping turds all the way, I followed with a pretend shovel, hoping to get a free ticket to the show for my efforts.

"Get outta here, kid," yelled one of men.

In the end, I got admitted in a very orthodox way — Mom paid.

"Willie wants a shampoo!" the clowns bellowed during their scintillating routine, and for a short while I was one happy kid, tucked away in the fifth row with a handful of chocolate, cotton candy, and my mother's hand. Yeah, that was a very good day.

Dad used to take me to afternoon westerns and cartoons at the local theatre, too, but I often had to leave because of my asthma attacks. The attacks were not without their small benefits though, and were worth an ice cream treat on my birthday.

One Christmas I became so excited at my "new" repainted tricycle that I lost my voice. Another time, more than once actually, I burst into tears at Christmas because I didn't think I'd given my parents enough. That type of reaction still happens. Depression and anxiety are not passing illnesses. As you can see, as soon as I think about two happy stories, I come up with a story of my Christmas anxiety. Maybe there just weren't enough happy times.

As a criminal lawyer, my dad had a brilliant mind, but he was chronically impatient. He had a fierce temper, crude country boy habits, and familiar fits. But the other side saw him regale the world with his boisterous stories, wear a morning suit with his OBE (Order of the British Empire) pinned dapperly on, and attend the elitist Queen's Garden Party. Everyone called him Ben. He was baptized Michael Bernard, but because of his hatred of the Catholic school system and the predators that ran it, he eschewed genuflection to Rome and curiously nodded toward Jerusalem with his nickname. But that's as far as it went. No egalitarian, my dad, his dislike of non-whites was awful. To him, the workmen who mended the broken roads were "Maori boys." They were never accorded the dignity of the correct use of the name — just Maori. And he called the local South Asian shoe repairer "the Nigger Boy." His was a different generation (not that that's any excuse).

Dad was Wellington's senior magistrate, and each day he would arrive home after work at exactly 5:00 p.m. For the next hour he would sit on a small, armless stool and lean against his classy, glassy, garish art deco cocktail cabinet and read *The Evening Post* to see if they were saying anything about him. Every few minutes he'd take a large belt of Laphroaig, his ten-year-old, single malt hammer of choice, with a squirt of soda water from a real gas-bomb-infused siphon. Every fifteen minutes he would call out to my mom, "Mary. More biscuits and cheese!"

The ritual continued on the weekends, but at the dinner table instead. "Get your bloody feet off the furniture!" he would yell. (Mahogany, you know.) He would then growl out an odd narration of his golf game of the day, which contained the most unusual verbal constructions: "Anyhow, there I was standing in the teeth of the gale," he would tell us, "and I slams one. I slams it beautifully. I takes out my putter. I strokes it. It rolls onto the side of the green and slides into the cup. Birdie two. A beauty. Then we goes on to the sixth."

This lasted exactly one hour. Dinner was at six. By that time, my dad was afire, his face glowing, yet his speech was hoarse and hostile. This was his time to berate the hell out of all of the family. We kids would drive him even nuttier by spinning our napkin rings across the table and watching them spin right back.

"Oh, for Christ sake, stop that!" he would say. "They're not bloody airplanes. Mary, make them stop it."

Dad's elderly mother also lived with us. One day Dad caught her scraping the skirting board with her shoes.

"Oh, Jesus Christ, you stupid old woman. Get your shoes off the bloody wood!"

Nanna, as we called her, burst into tears. Not that they were ever far away. Did she have depression genes, too? I think I see a pattern forming.

Then, every night at seven o'clock — yes, seven — Dad would go to bed and the house would become a sepulchre as his writ of silence engulfed us all. We were permitted quiet mumbles as my meek and subservient mother led us in the Roman Catholic rosary, but if I wanted to hear those new names in jazz — Miles Davis and someone called John Coltrane — I had to press my head against the radio speaker and hold it there for an hour. Any louder and I precipitated the wrath of Ben.

"Turn that bloody radio down!"

At least two of Dad's thirteen brothers had died of alcoholism as they battled the bleakness and privations of the post-Depression era, the years of the Second World War, and the rationing aftermath. During the war, Kiwi lives were often cut short, lost on alien soil fighting for condescending, monarchic leaders. The naive wanderlust of wild colonial boys found the adventure they had drooled about, but in the end they discovered that they were just cannon fodder — the Aussies and Canadians, too.

It was no wonder that few soldiers talked about their experiences after they came home. Not that they could have, even if they'd wanted to. They were told to shut up and take it. Be a man.

You're not crying are you? Jesus, mate, have another beer. No, better still, let's make it double vodka on the side. That'll set you right, mate.

But, of course, it didn't, ever. But it was all they had back then. They really did call depression "the blues"; or worse, the sufferers were labelled just plain crazy. The term *post-traumatic stress disorder* hadn't been invented yet. The condition was still referred to as shellshock.

I was about eight years old the first time I got hit with a standard twelve-inch wooden ruler.

Ah, blessings to you, Sister Claude.

Sister Claude was the newest entrant to the school. God knows what her real name was, but the original Saint Claude (a male) was an ascetic Jesuit in seventeenth-century France who once chillingly stated, "I have a terrible aversion for the life embraced."

Oh, happy days. Even back then, when mentally ill folks were judged to be just plain mad, Saint Claude's remark seems to indicate he was certainly suffering from depression. Sister Mary Claude (okay, for the non-Catholics, the *Mary* indicated a nun was a member of the paradoxically named Sisters of Mercy) had ferocious eyes, a lightly bearded chin, and reedy, whining vocal emanations. But she was little different from the rest of the traditionally dressed nuns who taught at St. Canice's primary school: yapping, snapping flocks of black and white gulls screeching over the white cliffs of Catholic morality.

Whack! Sit up straight.

Whack! You've got a spelling mistake.

Whack! You were talking in class.

I don't feel sorry for myself, but I knew no better. By the time I was twelve I had graduated to the cane. This was a little more sinister, considering the huge disease of pedophilia sweeping many denominations. We had a "Discipline Master" whom we nicknamed "Tubby" because of his hefty build. Tubby had a neat way of terrifying, humiliating, and inflicting excruciating pain on the students. Depending on his whim, a spelling mistake, absenteeism, talking, all got you up to three belts on either hand. The key was never to cry. Only sissies cried. So I guess I was a sissy. I got cane-whipped a number of times — the worst, the Tubby special. He made me take my pants down, underpants, too, bend well over, and wait.

Whack!

"Scully. What does *le jardin* mean?"

"I don't know, Father."

I wasn't very good at school, missing so many months as I had and never being able to catch up. My marks were always dreadful and I failed my first attempt at the New Zealand School Certificate; I was fifteen. However, there were strong indications that I was good at English and Theology, both subjects demanding original thinking.

Then, a year later, came my second chance at sitting the test, and this time I topped the entire country in English. Afterward, my teacher had just one question for me: "So what'd you do, Scully, cheat?"

Even back then, I remember my mood plummeting in unbearable disappointment. With those words, the dismissive teacher instantly obliterated my moment of pride. Today, I call these heavy bouts of depression "crashes." The stage for them was set in my school days.

When I got a bit older, to top things off, I was also shy. I was terrified of girls and seldom had the courage to ask one out. Instead, I'd usually get one of my mates to do it for me.

I didn't really discover girls until I was fourteen. I had a face festered with pimples, but dressed in the school uniform I looked crispy clean (though still frighteningly anxious) when I arrived to pick up my first date. It had been agony asking her out, but I had finally found a teaspoon of courage. Why her? She was pretty and had a glint in her eye when she spoke to me.

Andrea was twelve, two years younger than me. She was shy, five foot ten, gangly turning gorgeous, with peach-dappled skin and cheeky, sprouting breasts that thrust against her first bra. Her father was my dad's best friend at the Miramar Golf Club in Wellington. Scottish Mac, as he was correctly dubbed, was a club pro who had once qualified for the British Open. Both sets of parents felt that their kid was safe from the other.

The evening began when I met Andrea outside the old, ornate Majestic Theatre on Willis Street. She had on a below-the-knee blue cotton dress and short, white socks that stuck out of her Mary-Jane flats. Even I thought she was a bit young, but I bought us some chocolate and two ice creams. That was de rigueur in New Zealand at the time. Andrea licked her ice cream quickly. Maybe she hadn't had dinner — or maybe she was limbering up for greater things to come?

We went to see the smash musical hit *Picnic*, with the voluptuous Kim Novak pouring extra blood into the delivery system of every man in the cinema. When I gingerly leaned over to touch Andrea's hand, she snatched it away, either in fear or disgust. Or was it just coincidence? What did I know? I was fretting the entire time: *Should I try to put my arm around her? I wouldn't dare; I'm risking a smack in the head. Hand her a chocolate? Oh, give me a break, you idiot. You're too frightened to even hold her hand. Try to take her hand again? No, I'm too terrified to do it a second time. Oh, damn it. Damn it! Let's just get through the movie.*

It was 11:00 p.m. when we got off the city bus, walking a few feet apart, and I was desperately trying to think of a line that would either get her to kiss me or prompt her to go on another date. I didn't like my chances.

It just so happened that we both wore spectacles, and as we formalized a clumsy, fumbling good night grope, she suddenly bent down. I leaned in. *This was it! My first kiss! My, gosh, what's that happening to my what's-it?* In my excitement, I flipped my head around. Our glasses became entangled and flew to the ground.

No nookie that night. Not even for Ben's son.

I never saw Andrea again. I found the courage to phone her up the next day, but her parents said they'd rather she stayed at home. I don't know what she told them, but I hope they just thought I was too old for her — and not the town rapist. I went back to the pro shop every weekend for a while, but she was never there.

The morning after the date, my mom had asked me a strange question. "You're not doing anything naughty, are you?"

"No, Mom," I replied, somewhat puzzled.

"Well, I've got to wash the sheets, you know."

It wasn't until several years later that I understood my mom's embarrassing question.

I learned to play golf when I was about ten. I had professional coaching for several years after and was turning into quite a good player. In summer, my dad would take me to the course at six in the morning, and I would practise driving — both golf balls and the car. God knows what the other members thought, but I was Ben's boy, after all, wasn't I?

Memory plays odd tricks.

"And the winner of this year's New Zealand Junior Championship is John Scully."

New Zealand champion? Is that right? It might have been provincial champion. But no, it was club winner. But that's not bad, because New Zealand is a small place and I was up there near the top. And I did win a Parker pen as my prize. I could have used it to write about the unethical incident on the 15th hole. Let me explain.

I was doing okay, maybe looking like ending with an eighty-five that day. Miramar is a links course, sand and tussock by the sea. The rough was smooth on the dogleg 15th, and I hit a magnificent slice into the weeds that lived on the hill. My partners, three adults, went about their game, not paying much attention to the skinny kid with snow-white hair who stared with confusion at his scorecard, then wrote down the first number he thought of. On we went. Well, it wasn't as blatant as that, unless you discount the 15th.

The summer winds were blowing from the south as dark blotches of clouds scudded across the skyline. I went straight to where I had seen my ball land. *What the...?* It wasn't there. Oh, god, not a lost ball. It took forever to decide whether it had been lost or whether you had just cost yourself two strokes.

Ah! The ball! I found it wedged behind a tussock, with no way of getting a shot away. So with the innocence and insouciance of a drugged-up minor who didn't know all the rules of the game, I nonchalantly tapped the ball with my foot a couple of times until I got a better lie from which to hit it. Nobody saw me — except Andrea's dad. When I came into the clubhouse and handed him my scorecard, he looked and looked and looked.

"Johnnie, what's this here on the 15th?"

"Oh, I lost my ball. I didn't know how to mark the card, so I put down "x.""

"I see. Well, leave the card with me, Johnnie."

Two weeks later, the mailman delivered a white, official-looking envelope. I ripped it open and read: "Dear John Scully, The executive committee of the Miramar Golf Club is happy to announce that you have won the championship."

I won? What? What had her dad done?

I had committed a mortal sin of golf. Now, that really would have been time for confession; but I didn't do that anymore. So I just took the championship fountain pen that was enclosed and ran.

The rest of my sports career could best be described by one word: *depressing.* This was likely influential in my later mood crashes.

I was officially a rugby "midget" at the age of ten, and even played for the Wellington provincial midget team in a curtain raiser for a big international match. The crowd was supportive (and drunk) and left en masse when our game was over. As if!

John's rugby team, Grade 3. John is seated in the front row, far right.

There's a ground in Wellington, cruelly called Martin Luckie Park (lucky, my ass!). Our enemies that day were a team from the secular Rongotai College. We were at the sideline about halfway down the field as the ball was thrown into play. Rongotai snatched it and the halfback hurled the ball on to a colleague. Except I intercepted the pass and ran like hell for fifty yards, our team and my dad cheering me on to a certain try. I slowed as I neared the five-yard line, the four, the three, the two, the one, and then the culmination of this sensational sequence. But when I bent over to touch the ball down to make it legal, I dropped it.

A few weeks later, all the rugby players ran from school through the Hataitai Tunnel to the training ground. Sprints, jumps, and tackles loosened us up before playing a practice game with another school team. One of my favourite players was a guy named Al, who introduced himself in a very aggressive manner — he head-butted me. Accidently, of course.

Whack!

Jesus, the pain!

"Scully, does your nose always reach to your eye?" inquired the trained observer of a priest who'd seen me throughout the time I was at school. Blood poured out all the way to the hospital, where they put me under to repair my squashed and badly broken nose.

No more rugby for Johnnie.

It is still hard on me to remember the bewildering events at the school sports meetings. Athletically, I was a nobody, always an also-ran. Even so, they once stuck me in two races with the top runners in the 100 and 220 yards, I think to fill out the lanes.

Bang!

My little bare feet spun as fast as I could make them go, and normally it was never enough. But that day, as I rounded the bend, I thought *Huh?* I was five yards ahead of the best athletes in the school. To this day, I don't know how my gears kicked in, but the fallout was, well, dramatic.

The girls from Sacred Heart College had their own goals. They would hunt for the hunks that were doing all the winning at athletics that day. Curiously, the very short-skirted, good Catholic girls weren't interested in the Yellow Flash — me, wearing a brilliant yellow turtleneck sweater as warm-up gear. I looked like scrambled eggs with legs.

Mom and Dad had come to see me make my first start as a track star in the 220 yards. When it came to starting time, I transmogrified into a real Olympian — the big threat. Underneath my scrambled egg sweater I wore the official blue and white uniform of our top athletics team. It made me feel as if I had won the gold already. I borrowed my nose-breaking friend's running shoes, and jumped, sprinted, and bounced on the spot at the track of our great rivals, St. Patrick's College, a boarding school about twenty kilometres from our school in Wellington. This was going to be a walkover.

I had drawn lane four.

"Take your marks!"

I glanced up, I looked ahead, then down at the start line, then over at the starter.

No sign of asthma.

"Settle down, lane four!"

Who? Me?

"Set!"

All the runners were down in the traditional crouched start. Except me; I didn't know how to do it, so I pretended.

The guy in lane seven blessed himself. Good thinking; he'd need all the help he could get against me, I thought. The starter almost religiously raised the gun.

Don't try to guess the start. Wait. Wait.

Bang!

I took off free and easy, fast, running in a beautiful rhythm. It felt so good. As we rounded the bend and I straightened up for the surge to the winning tape, I could see Mom and Dad cheering me on at the finish line. Spectacular!

But wait a minute. What the hell? Where are the other runners? What? They've all finished?

I was last by thirty yards. That did it for competitive running for me. I switched to the long jump. Huh! Long jump! More like an extremely short jump. That didn't get me onto the athletics team. Nothing ever did again.

My first sex?

Oh dear, oh dear, oh dear. Must I? I wouldn't mention it, except that my self-esteem issues continue to plague me in that area.

I didn't get that chat from my parents, so even at the age of nineteen I was unclear about what was supposed to happen between my erection and whatever was between a woman's legs. Still, Sarah was my tour guide. I met her in the photo department at the *Evening Post*. She had big, um, I think we brazenly called them tits, and she seemed to know her way artfully around the male and female forms. Back at her place, she undid her bra and daringly showed me her bulbous breasts. She placed my hands on her hard, erect nipples. *Oh boy, did I like that!* Then she put her hands on my penis and told me to put it in. But, in a scene with which I would become depressingly familiar, everything happened too soon.

Bill, Sarah's brother burst on this embarrassing scene, said he'd tell his mum, and left. I never heard from Sarah's brother (or mother) again, and I only saw Sarah occasionally at work. But I continued to chase my dream. Too many Catholic virgins — or so they told me — went through the motions of refusing close physical contact. Many of them meant it. But eventually I found some willing participants — sexually aggressive, patient, tutorial schoolgirls with the accelerator squeezed all the way down. Of course, after a time I became one of the best Kiwi lovers in history, you know — New Zealand's number one stud.

9

CUB REPORTER PAR (NOT SO) EXCELLENCE

When I was sixteen, my dad got me a summer job in the *Evening Post* pressroom. The school had said I was too dumb to go to university and study medicine, so my parents decided to put me in a trade. At the end of the first day, the head pressman came over to me.

"Are you the Scully boy?" he asked.

"Yes."

"Well, we don't need you, so I'm giving you to Charlie, the illustrations editor. He needs someone to file the picture blocks of dead New Zealanders."

Charlie was a nice guy, and I liked being around the photographs. But then came the day he wanted his lunch. He didn't have time to go to the cafeteria because of noon deadlines.

"Johnnie, could you please go and get me my ham sandwich from the caf. Mrs. Billings has it ready. Here's ten shillings. That's ham, Johnnie."

"Right-o. She'll be right."

And off I went to the cafeteria.

"Oh, John. You're here for Charlie's sandwich?"

"Yes, Mrs. Billings."

"Well, I've got two left. You might as well take them."

What nobody told me was that the second bloody sandwich had been promised to Graeme, the chief sub-editor. I ate his entire ham sandwich.

When I realized this, I dropped Charlie's sandwich on his desk and ran like hell.

Oh, Jesus, what have I done? I thought.

In my mind this was a catastrophe. I was so terrified that I wouldn't go back to the paper six months later when the next school holiday arrived. When I finally phoned Charlie and confessed my awful deed, he laughed, puzzled, and professed no memory whatsoever of my theft of the ham sandwich.

But right there were four, count them, four huge signs blasting away in brilliant neon if anyone, including me, had bothered to really look at my moods: terror, shame, fear, and unrelenting guilt, all symptoms of depression and anxiety. Other signs wouldn't appear for a while, but when they did, disaster hit.

Jump!

A frightening word for me. It's called acrophobia, and it's a fear of heights. I bet you didn't know that many people with severe depression suffer from it. The same goes for eczema. And I have them both. The acrophobia gave me the dizzying, terrifying fear I was going to crash and crumple; my brain spun when I looked over the side of a precipice. And the nausea! It felt as if a magnet was pulling me down at blinding speed. *Am I safe? Am I dead?*

One day, Charlie had an assignment for me.

"Johnnie, do you see the scaffolding high up on that building site?"

"Yeah. You mean that scaffold through the back window here?"

"Wouldn't it make a great picture if you went to the very end of the girder and composed a shot with that New Zealand flag in the foreground and the rest of the city below? Do you think you can do it?"

"Yes," I lied, horrified.

What Charlie didn't mention was that there was no safety equipment — no helmets, no belts — just my camera and me. It was suicidal, stupid. Yet, I still went ahead.

As I climbed, girder after girder and higher and higher, I looked down. *Oh, holy shit!* The street far below grabbed me and tried to suck me into its grave. My legs wobbled and vibrated as the regular workers laughed and laughed at the half-bent figure carrying two cameras around his neck, the equipment smashing against the girders all the way.

I had one more girder to go when I suddenly thought *I can't do it.* About five metres of steel and a sheer drop fell away on either side of me. I was stuck. I couldn't move.

But I had to. Charlie wanted his flag shot, so I had to get it: F8 at one-hundredth of a second. Or was it F100 at one-eighth? Who the hell knows?

The cameras were all manual, which meant I had to use both hands to set them.

Look, Charlie, no hands.

I snapped off half a dozen shots before I slipped off the girder, sliding and scraping roughly back to earth. I quickly hustled to the lavatory to empty my exceedingly loose bowels.

Another day, Charlie called me over.

"Johnnie, I've got a great assignment for you," he enthused.

"You mean the Beatles?"

"Yeah, I want a front page spread of them. Neil, Ian, and Merv are posted along the route in from the airport to the St. George Hotel. But I want you to have a chance at a cover. Take the yellow Volkswagen. You might need it for a quick getaway."

The hotel was just around the corner, but if Charlie said take the car, I'd take the car.

For Wellington, the crowds outside the Hotel St. George were phenomenal. It was mainly teenage and younger girls screeching and crooning for their loved ones, and as the four young men crammed onto the hotel balcony, the panties started flying. This same scene had been played out on newsreels around the world.

I swung the VW to the right, and there they were — the Fab Four — waving and swaying to the background music. I almost hit four fans as I tried to get closer.

Wait. Get back out of this, I thought. There would be a great shot from the edge of the crowd.

Paul was wringing this one for all he could get. It had been at least twelve hours since his last dose of adulation. He needed more. I swung the car back in the opposite direction and bumped and grinded my way to the edge. There it was, the front-page shot Charlie was counting on: massive lunchtime crowds swarming the Hotel St. George. The shot from the outer edge was going to be spectacular: Beatles in the background, thousands of screaming fans in the foreground.

I hustled around the front of the car to get out the tripod and a battery. All set up. *That was fast! Now where's my shot? What the …? Where's my fucking shot?*

It's over, sunshine.

While I was setting up the tripod, the boys had slipped back into the hotel and were not seen again that day. Security made sure of that.

Six months later, Charlie gave me another chance, this time in the world of sports.

It was nine in the morning when I got my orders: Get a picture of Lew Hoad, one of the best tennis players alive, and don't let anything stop you.

Okay.

So I walked over to the hotel where Hoad was staying and luckily ran into his manager, Harry Miller, an entrepreneur in town who I knew. "Harry, I need a picture of Lew. Where is he?"

"I think he's still in his room. Wait here and I'll go and see."

Don't let anything stop you, Charlie had said.

I slipped into the elevator with Harry, who had a key to the champion's room.

"Okay, John, but don't do anything to upset Lew."

"No, of course not. I wouldn't do that."

When the elevator stopped at the right floor, we got off together.

"Wait here and I'll see if he's up," Harry told me.

But I didn't wait, and I dashed into the small room. Hoad was fast asleep, but I started shooting pictures with the flash. That woke him up. I took one more picture.

Boy was he mad!

Still, I got Charlie his picture, even if I was told to fuck off by the world's greatest tennis player.

The *Post*'s pop critic reviewed the concerts, but when the guy doing the job started to become too busy as a street reporter, I took over many of the music review beats. Suddenly, the giants of music began to appear before me. There was Igor Stravinsky with his soft hands and his shimmering, blasting version of *The Firebird*, the likes of which had never been heard before in Wellington. Miles Davis didn't say much to me, just "Hi, kid." Pop singer Dusty Springfield was light, funny, and seemingly happy — she hadn't come out yet. Guitar genius Andres Segovia was a gentleman, but moved quickly on. Ella Fitzgerald was chatty and friendly, talking about the weather and the hall before heading back to practise with Dizzy Gillespie and his big band. And then there was the great Sarah Vaughan. What a bitch, but one of the most brilliant jazz singers of any era.

"Sarah, I'd like you to meet our top concert critic, John Scully."

"Yeah." And with that, she turned her back and continued pitching scales.

In one newspaper review, I insolently criticized Dave Brubeck and his Quartet as "pure ham," although the next morning I did see Brubeck's great alto sax player, Paul Desmond, wandering lonely as a shroud down Willis Street. I didn't have the courage to cross over and say "Gidday." Why? The "pure ham" comment was over the top. I had written it to be cheeky. It was a good journalistic lesson: be fair.

About that time, I joined the Victoria University Jazz Club. I had bought myself a tenor saxophone, and since all my friends were at university, I tagged along with them. I was the world's worst tenor player (and the worst oboe and flute player, as well). But I loved it. Breathing

John with his tenor sax, age twenty.

was of little problem with the woodwinds, but I just wished I could play the fucking things. I was humiliated with an intolerable lack of self-esteem. I practised day and night, but to no avail. I was still ejected from three bandstands that I recall. I had too much trouble reading the scores.

One night we played the University Jazz Club, and a would-be experimental jazz singer named Margo Sutherland wanted me to start my tenor sax solo wailing and stuttering and screaming — all very Ornette Coleman. The lights were down as I softly, then quickly built to a crescendo, and Margo became Annie Ross. The lights came up and I walked, playing, to the centre of the stage. Margo kept up her vocals. We nodded to each other and, as planned, Margo stepped forward and I stepped back — and straight down a huge hole in the floor of the darkened backstage area. My mouth was all cut and bloodied, my saxophone was broken, and my ego was crushed.

Even so, life continued and on occasion was surprising.

"Hey, Johnnie," enthused Charlie a couple of months later, "*The Sports Post* wants help with their new edition." (*The Sports Post* came out every Saturday evening with all the latest sports news and results.)

"What? Last minute stories and so on?"

"No, Johnnie. We've heard you whistle all the time and noticed you've got an ear for music. So we want you to write a record review column."

"Wow. Sure!"

"Now, we need a hip name for it," he said.

"How about Platter Chatter?" I suggested.

"Platter Chatter! That's great! Very hip."

Yes, a truly great title, but ever since I have denied that I had anything to do with it.

10

THE BBC AND OTHER STORIES

When I was twenty-two, I left the *Post* and joined Radio New Zealand as a reporter. The prize for this inspired move was the morning shift. When they said *morning*, I thought they meant 8:00 a.m. to 5:00 p.m.

"So, Scully, I'll pick you up in my taxi at half past three."

"In the morning?"

"Yes. The shift starts at four."

My boss in the taxi was Bob, a wizened, crinkled, grumpy alcoholic who didn't talk much.

My first job was to monitor overseas radio news and write up any story I thought of interest. A couple of my more memorable lines of morning shift journalism included "The Vatican is making big changes to the Cistern Chapel" and — possibly the greatest line of all time, which I sent as a news flash to all RNZ's stations — "It's one small step for man, one small step for mankind."

And guess who happened to be visiting the newsroom the day I spoke the latter? The head of news at the British Broadcasting Corporation. He stayed around for a week, during which time I was switched to TV duty.

Something about me impressed him — my lovely blond hair, the boils in my ears? I'm not sure what, but whatever it was, I got the call: "John, why don't you come back to London with me and work for the BBC?"

Before he could finish the sentence, I had accepted.

Before I left for England, I had one very important thing to do: I got married. I had met my wife, Toni, when she was a dance teacher and professional jeweller. I thought she was a wonderful, great-looking woman, and still do. (Remarkably, we still live together after forty-eight years of marriage.)

Even back in the earlier days I was consumed by my career. So the day after our wedding, we packed up and left on a six-week voyage to England on the *Fairsky*. (This was just before the jet passenger age.) On the way, the ship stopped at magical foreign ports like Singapore, Suez, Cairo, Aden, and Naples. It was my first trip abroad and I was blown away. As for the honeymoon, it was as romantic as it gets.

But after six weeks of bliss, I experienced a rude awakening when we arrived in London.

The BBC I joined was housed in the eastern end of the thrice-rebuilt "Ally Pally," as Alexandra Palace was known to everyone at the time. The palace had been the Beeb's transmitting centre for more than fifty years, and it was from there that the first public television transmission had hit the air back in 1936. It had a "club" — an in-house watering hole — on the premises and, even more dangerous, an outdoor tin shack where all the heavy drinkers spent their lunch hour. The number of identifiable alcoholics at the time was quite high.

After my shaky start as a colonial rewrite producer, then summer relief, and finally temporary fill-in for a six-week trial, they decided to keep me on. After I was officially hired, they sent me to school — BBC style.

I tentatively tripped down the two flights of stairs in the tower, across a grim, ill-lit garage, and into the light: the BBC Training Centre. Journalism boot camp, ten hours a day for fourteen weeks.

This was reputedly the best and toughest training course for journalists in the world. If you could cut it there, you could not only beat out the

John and Toni's wedding, May 4, 1965.

Relaxing aboard the SS Fairsky *during the six-week voyage from New Zealand to London, May 1965.*

competitors, but often broadcast the best TV news and current affairs in the Western world. And it all started with a ruthless and impassioned belief in truth and technique.

The bosses at the BBC were unrelenting and utterly unforgiving. The course was intense, and it pushed me to my limits. But I mercifully responded, leaving even the Oxbridge grads in the evening mist.

"We broadcast at how many words?" barked the trainer.

Silence.

"Okay. This is the rule. Not a whim, it's a rule. BBC broadcasters speak at three words a second."

He was unrelenting.

"A political hot potato? Who in the fuck wrote that? It's one of the worst clichés in our vocabulary. Clichés are out. Gone. Dead. Use them at your peril…. What do you mean it *might* happen? So my ass *might* catch fire? There's no such thing as *might*. Find the truth. That has the might you're looking for."

It was unspoken, but for all the guys on trial, this was our big (and maybe only) chance.

On the training course were several senior reporters — the big names, one of whom couldn't stand any of the BBC's pictures-before-words nonsense. He was reddening by the hour as he became less and less tolerant. And how did our hero deal with his anxiety and anger? Well, one morning they wouldn't let him into the car park because he had been rude to the gatekeeper, and the black and white barrier stayed locked in place.

"Raise that fucking thing or I'll mow you down!" he yelled out the window of the car.

And so he did. He smashed his car into the barrier, hit the gatekeeper, and later faced a police investigation. In the end, his punishment at the BBC was serving time as an in-house producer — no trips, and no stories with his face plastered all over them.

Such were the stresses and intractable demands of the training course.

I wonder if that was when my unintended depression cover-up began. The adrenalin would start pumping; my brain would be seized with the certainty of the BBC and its form of absolutism journalism. I had to be right. I had to be first. I had to be the best. I didn't have time to feel depressed. And it's likely this carried me through most of my career, as I buried my illness in not so fanciful flights to the war zones and shitholes of the world at the time, like Belfast (at least two dozen times), the Middle East, and Central America. There was no depression in the air when I was on assignment; that didn't hit me until I got home. But it was never long before I was fired out of the cannon once again.

After two years at the BBC, I was sent to the advanced film directors and film editors course. At that time I was working as a writer, but I was already making my way up through the system, backing up the foreign editor.

The BBC was insistent that we must be aware of every picture and visual nuance — that we could write to any picture, write any story, no matter the deadline. And we had to get it right. A tough job, but it's what TV stations did in North America.

The story that solidified my place at the BBC as a world "heavyweight" was, poetically, about outer space. I was producing the corporation's coverage of all the Apollo moon shots. The BBC training system had convinced me to … no, implicitly demanded that I read and remember every page in the Apollo pilot's flight manual. So I sat in Kensington Gardens for four hours and memorized, and understood, this most technical of manuals. Hell, they'd once made me learn the rules of cricket, so this should be a breeze! It was this drive and demand for perfection that forced me to learn as much about the flights as the astronauts. I reckon I could have flown the capsule myself. It was crazy.

But that was the job: Give the BBC what they demanded — the impossible. And you'd better deliver to the highest ideals of television journalism.

But here's the real scoop. During the Apollo moon shots, I helped develop a new way of editing the old one-inch videotape of the moonwalks, and because of my training, when disaster hit Apollo 13, I had the confidence, and the news sharpness developed by the training system, to put it on the air ahead of NASA's famous: "Houston, we have a problem."

I'm told I was the first in the world to break the story. I was on my way up and up.

But in a few hours I, too, would have a problem. Throughout the day we ran news specials culminating with the main nine o'clock news. It had been a triumphant day. I had to stay behind to re-edit the Apollo story for the late news. By the time I'd finished, it was 11:15 p.m. The bar was closed and everyone had gone home. The place was utterly deserted.

In the BBC newsroom, London, 1966.

On my desk lay the detritus of forty days and nights of covering the mission — old scripts, maps, charts, the manual. A couple of ballpoint pens lay in the corner next to the earphones from which a NASA man still crackled his incessant space-speak.

"It was a day like no other," they had told me. "You did an incredible job," they said. But as I gazed at the emptiness, for the first time I felt far from elated. In fact, I had a sudden emotional flop, something I would become more familiar with as I got older. I felt desolate, disappointed, saddened, and oh so empty. And I forlornly asked myself, *Is that it? Is that all there is?*

During one BBC training session, I became the Orson Welles of Ally Pally, with his Magnificent Seven, seven being the number of men and women on the crew I was to use.

Before I came to London, a TV New Zealand crew was comprised of a film camera and, if you were lucky, a soundman. I had all of a year in television before going to the Beeb. At the BBC, a crew consisted of a camera operator, an assistant, a sound person, an electrician, a production assistant, a producer, and, yes, a driver. The course was run by the leaders of cinematography in the U.K. We studied Sidney Lumet's *The Hill* and were introduced to the notions of continuity, silence, shadows, drama, structure, and other strict rules of shooting and editing. These lessons came from Britain's finest. What a treat.

Our training brief was simple: "Here's a crew of seven people. Go out and make a three-minute feature incorporating all you have learned. The subject doesn't matter. The content doesn't matter. What does matter is have you mastered visual literacy?" (By the way, on the cameraman's test, they had to shoot one street sign from twenty-six angles!)

What to do with a crew of seven? Well, I decided to go all arty and made a short film in Epping Tube Station. As a train, massively compressed into slow motion, snaked endlessly toward the camera, on the platform I had a model in a diaphanous (well, almost pornographic) gown turning in synchronization as a narrator recited lines from a Yeats poem: "Turning, turning in the widening gyre."

I know, it sounds like crap, but it worked and the trainers liked it a lot. *Phew!* And the model in the pink see-through gown? I was tempted to offer her training lessons of my own, but she saw right through my pathetic ruse and, after receiving her performance cheque, told me to fuck off. Can't say I blame her. Oh, yeah, the soundtrack I used? It had to be Miles Davis and his mood-clutching "In a Silent Way." The trainer liked the precise way the film was edited and the sparing use of music. Again, for Miles fans, it was my kind of "Seven Steps to Heaven."

When it became clear that I was lacking in my knowledge of British society, I decided to do some extra training on my own. I attended London School of Economics University-sponsored seminars and did a year or so involved with the school itself, this time distance learning. My subjects? Economics, British Constitution, and Economic History — all exceedingly boring, but invaluable.

As I moved up the newsroom chain (the youngest duty editor in BBC history, I'm told), my suited, tied, and plummy superiors assigned me to redesign the flagship newscast, *The BBC Nine O'Clock News*. When my design was accepted, I was seen as yet another success, another one of their "golden boys."

But not everything glittered at the time.

Problems. For me? Could it be possible? Not for the boy wonder with the long hair and floral shirts, surely?

Well, I got the name of a town wrong on a map once after having a pint of beer at lunch. I was abused and pilloried before the entire newsroom in a brutal, ugly lesson I will never forget, all because of one tiny spelling mistake. That experience has served me well to this day, though, and since that excoriation, I've never had even a drop of booze at lunch when I'm working.

It was about that time that I began covering in-depth the events plaguing Northern Ireland. I even went there on Christmas Day because no one else would. The story was always more important than my family. I had to keep moving and working — New Year's, birthdays, anniversaries, kids' plays.

Looking back, it was pathetic and sad. But was the depression to blame, or was it my insatiable addiction to covering news and current affairs? Or was it a bit of both? Whatever the conclusion, I'm not proud of the way I treated my family at that time — disgusted with myself, in fact.

But would I do it again? Oh, god, I don't know. I do know that this journalistic fire inside me was stoked heavily every day by the BBC. It was a cerebral commitment they demanded, not just fast turnarounds and flashy field and newsroom antics: "Dear boy, think! Think before you act. In the newsroom or in the field. I don't want gratuitous violence. I want the story. The truth. Balanced. With pictures and sound. Got that?"

That was perhaps the greatest lesson I ever learned. *Think. Join the dots. Don't believe anyone.* As one BBC anchor said of his interview style with politicians, "I want to know why this lying bastard is lying to me."

No compromise and, if I may, no surrender.

And so it continued, with more training outside of the newsroom in the form of dozens more trips to mean, vicious Belfast as the national news editor. Death threats, car bombs, assassinations; I was even in the BBC itself, a fortress built in the 1940s, when a bomb exploded outside. The building shook, rattled, heaved, and echoed, but in the end withstood the powerful blast, probably set by the Protestant Ulster Defence Association. But who knows? I remember looking out of the window and thinking *Oh, God.* The building opposite had been hit. Workers were flooding out, screaming. The death toll was irrelevant. It was terror they were seeking.

To compound things, at the time I was also the number two man in charge of the *BBC National TV News* in London. It was a job in which incessant stress and exploding nerves disguised any overt signs of my depression.

What journalists call a "big break" came for me in 1967 when I was sent to Bangladesh to do an "instant documentary" about the East Pakistan war and the endless columns of refugees dying in a cholera epidemic. About two kilometres from the border, there was a smell that became an emetic stench. The sweet, sickly, gut-throwing smell of decayed bodies lying in a refugee camp permeated the humid air. Vultures pecked at the dozens of unburied bodies as children tried to stop them from eating their dead parents. A vile pond served both as drinking water and toilet. I saw two men drinking from the green scum while another urinated into it and a woman vomited violently nearby.

Mixed in with the smell of death was something else. I accidentally stepped into a grassed area that, unknown to me, was being used as a massive toilet. I sank ankle-deep into the putrid muck and dry-heaved for a least a minute: gone, one more pair of boots and jeans.

Back in the camp, as usual, humble, penniless refugees offered me a cup of tea. I couldn't refuse, but I had made it a rule never to drink untreated water, so I put it behind my back and, in a well-practised routine, poured it out surreptitiously.

The images I witnessed first-hand in Bangladesh were so grotesque that they still remain firmly embedded somewhere in my brain. My depression was under control, but it couldn't survive the daunting mental challenge I was subjecting myself to.

I returned to Bangladesh, this time to cover the famine. The images of skeletons moaning and death haunt me to this day. That was the beginning of my battle with post-traumatic stress disorder.

At that time, I was acting senior editor, but when the producer's job in Washington was posted, I wanted it badly. It would be the chance to experience a different culture, to cover different stories; plus it was a higher job grade and, as a result, promised more money.

My colleagues had no doubts: My boss said, "Scully, it's yours. You can't miss."

But the BBC interview board had other ideas, and I was rejected. When I first opened the envelope informing me of the disastrous news, I thought I must have performed badly in the interview. I was sick, unbelieving; egotistically incredulous. It was then that a distant echo of something I didn't yet recognize started up — a nasty, despairing thunder of a state of mind that I was unfamiliar with. I remember sloughing across the road to the tube station and just staring at the rails for ten minutes — trains screaming to a stop and grinding off again, nothing more.

Why didn't I get the job?

Instead, it had gone to a guy whose main purpose in life seemed to be selling coloured ties made by his wife. A shit-disturbing security reporter I knew later provided one version of the truth: he figured that a couple of us new boys had been "red carded." According to the reporter, that meant we had been tagged with two great sins that would prevent us from receiving any further promotions: First, we were from the colonies, not from one of their great universities. Second, privately some of us expressed our support for the goals of the IRA.

Was there any truth in this explanation? I don't know. But I do know the class system showed its repulsive side too often at the BBC. Political correctness had not yet been invented: Women were typists. Smoking in the newsroom was common.

We newbies confused ourselves in a variety of ways that added credence to the BBC's alleged argument about the IRA. For example, around that time, one young reporter was sent to Londonderry to make another documentary on "The Troubles." He was there for a week. During that time he was hit by a couple of rubber bullets, but otherwise survived the abuse of the lads wrapped in the Irish tri-colour of green, white, and orange. He became one of the few pleasant notes from Northern Ireland: not one journalist was killed directly as a result of that violence. It was gang versus gang, thug versus thug, assassin versus assassin; a world of spies, hit men, and army brutality.

So our newbie flag-bearer returned to London and entered the "truth factory" — a film editing suite where, heart in mouth, you would see for the first time what pictures and sound you got — or

In the BBC newsroom, London, 1973.

worse, discover a vital sequence that you missed. The film was scheduled to run the next night. Suddenly, a shouting match echoed up from the floor below. It seemed the editor, the big boss, was more than a little underwhelmed.

"What the fuck is this?" he yelled. "It's all fucking IRA propaganda. The BBC can't run anything like this! Jesus Christ. It's useless. Drop it. "

They kept a very close eye on us new boys when it came to long-form journalism, and they learned from that lesson about planning and briefing. It wasn't all my colleague's fault. His brief was vague. He was new. But the BBC swore it would not allow anything like that to happen again. Christ, it might have gone to air and we'd have a new round of madness from all the rioters watching themselves on the *Six O'Clock News*.

It was while I was at the BBC that Toni and I started having marital problems. I didn't realize it for what it was at the time, but I had a huge depression crash the day Toni and I split up and she took my son, Jerome, then two years old, back to New Zealand. I cried convulsively for several days. I was crippled by sadness beyond any I'd previous experienced.

The loneliness, self-pity, and despair went on for month after month. I was still a star in the newsroom and beyond, so nobody noticed at work, or if they did notice they were too stigmatized to mention that I seemed down. I recall that one person described me as "manic," which suggests bipolar disorder.

But professionally, I felt that there was nothing I couldn't do. That's why, I think, no one suspected depression. I was so confident about my work, and my depression and anxiety were still heavily disguised by my obsession with my job. Certainly the BBC doctor didn't detect anything, nor did my own GP or any London specialist. In their minds, I just had a preponderance to drink too much alcohol. After a twelve-hour shift, I would regularly join my colleagues in the BBC bar and drink two or three pints of Stella Artois chased down with several Irish whiskies. I was developing a booze habit.

11

THE MOVE TO CANADA

"I am not a crook!"

But President Nixon *was* a crook, and the BBC sent me to Washington to produce coverage of the Watergate break-in.

One day, the phone in my Georgetown hotel rang.

"Is that John Scully from the BBC?"

"Yes. Who is this?"

It was the head of a new Canadian television network.

"I'm calling from Toronto. I'm putting together a news team for the new Global TV Network. I've heard all about you and I wonder if you'd be interested in being the senior field producer?"

"Not really. I like the BBC."

"I understand. A great outfit. But John, let me tell you that goin' down the road this place is gonna make a piss pot full of money."

"Ah, I need to think about it," I told him.

"Why don't you drop by Toronto on your way back to London and we can have a chat? Just a chat," he assured me.

By that point, Toni and I had reconciled and we now had two children, Jerome and Emma. The financial pressures on us were heavy. It may surprise you that a family of four had a hard time making ends meet in London on a BBC journalist's salary, but it's true. We didn't have a lot of meat in our meals, we had a beat-up car, and the kids' clothing was expensive. The fact was that British salaries just had not caught up with those in North America.

So, basically, I sold out. I resigned from the BBC and moved to Canada. What can I say? They offered me a lot of money. Well, it seemed like a lot to me at the time. It was a great move: Global went into receivership six weeks later.

Fuck!

So there I was, stranded in Canada, my family still in London, and my job about to end. This happened not long after Christmas 1973. On Christmas Day, I found myself alone in a hotel room, and I cried for most of the day. Maybe I wasn't as stable as I thought.

Thankfully, some financial genius found a way to get Global TV out of receivership, and I ended up working there for the next four years. I covered wars, uprisings, demonstrations, and riots in places like Vietnam, Beirut, and Northern Ireland. In the end, it turned out to be one of the better periods of my life. On the superficial side, I was making more money than the average Kiwi, British, or even Canadian journalist. Toni and I had a big four-bedroom house on a classy Toronto street and we had a huge car — a big blue Matador. We had steak when we wanted, a fridge full of beer and wine, and cognac in the cupboard. We hosted lots of parties with colleagues. Apparently, there was lots of laughter. I say *apparently* because, guess what, I can't remember a lot of those good times.

It's one of my problems. I seem to forget the better times. Do I repress them? Can I not accept the fact I had fun? Was I even really having fun, even though friends and relatives tell me I was? The truth is, I just don't remember.

I do remember we had some excellent journalists at Global. I was hired to make those good journalists better and the weak journalists acceptable. And I think I did a pretty good job. My kids tell me I was relatively happy then, though obsessed. Jerome and Emma remember that it would take me a full week to come down after returning from a trip covering a war.

Along with Toni, my kids kept me from mentally crashing during that period. They do the same today. Without Toni, I would not be here. I don't mean I wouldn't be here writing; I mean I wouldn't be here on this planet. Toni is my lifeline. And Liam, my five-year-old grandson, plays an important role also. He gives me unconditional joy. And it's reciprocal. Did I just use the word *joy*? I guess I did. Unfortunately, Liam wasn't around back then, during the "good old days."

I must confess that when I was in my mid-thirties working in Canada, I did increase my reliance on drugs. Usually called uppers and downers, what I really took were sleeping pills to relax and a form of speed to get me going. There was a lot of booze during those years, too, but I don't think you would call me an alcoholic. As a parent, was I as overbearing as my father? Apparently not. But guess what? It did not even occur to me then. The job still came first.

But then my moods started to go up and down.

One of my favourite Global TV stories is about covering a fire. You know how journalists are often called fire-chasers? Well, on that particular day, a flapping grey rotor blade was clattering through miles of smoke and haze as firefighters tried to drench a huge forest fire in western Ontario. On board our chopper were three of the great firefighters of our generation, a reporter, a cameraman, and me. Oh, yeah, and a pilot. We were searching for a place to land amid the flames. I had wanted the reporter to perform a very rushed piece to camera surrounded by the burning forest. We had arranged that after the chopper dropped us, it would fly off because it was too dangerous to hang around. It would return to pick us up after four minutes exactly, ready or not. Otherwise, it would be in danger of running out of gas.

After landing, we jumped out of the chopper with the most basic of camera and audio equipment. It always takes a minute or so to get the shot right, and when we had three minutes left, the reporter started: "There's no more ... oh Jesus! Sorry guys. I forgot my lines."

We regrouped.

"Go again! Now! The chopper'll be back in one minute!"

There we were, in the chaos and frenzy, standing in the midst of a flaming circle, with hardly enough time for one more take. The flames were, at most, thirty metres away. And in that scorching, blinding fire, with only seconds left, here's what the reporter blurted out: "I'm standing as close to the gates of hell as a man dare."

"Jesus, fuck, Colin. That's nonsense. Go again. Where you are and why. Oh fuck! That sounds like the chopper."

Yep. From that life-threatening attempt at a spectacular piece to camera, your heroes came away from "the gates of hell" with, wait for it, not a thing. I inquired about the laws of manslaughter before attempting to throw the reporter out of the chopper at six thousand feet.

Professional depression is almost as bad as the real thing. The chopper dropped us back at a parking lot and we jumped in the car and headed for the main road. Suddenly, we were engulfed by smoke and licks of flame; the fire was in front of us and behind us. The reporter, who was driving, rolled the dice, gunned the engine, and we careened through the calamity and came out safely on the other side.

I turned to the cameraman. "That must have made some great footage, eh?"

"Oh. You wanted me to roll on that?" he said.

Later, the chief firefighter decided he'd had enough of me and my whining, demanding transportation, and being a general pain in the ass, and he phoned the assignment desk to officially complain, calling me "the most arrogant man it has been my displeasure to meet." However, he did concede that, "even so, I gotta say he produced the best fire story I've ever seen."

Global was finally doing well. In fact, in 1977 our ratings in Toronto had grown stronger than the CBC's. The network was on a roll. There was money to be made and money to be spent. One of the ways they spent it was by throwing a big Christmas party. They gave everyone tickets for a couple of free drinks, and cheap drinks were available for those of us who wanted more. Most of us had a few too many, and the party got a bit wild as work friends of ours won television sets and radios in the draws. I continued to take advantage of the cheap drinks.

The party took place a week before Christmas and a couple of weeks after I had done a good job with a fairly inexperienced reporter on his first assignment to Belfast. Not only had the boss of news complimented the reporter and me on our work, but the president of the company had come around to the newsroom, searched us out at our desks, and shaken our hands. It may not seem like much, but television company presidents don't usually do that, especially in front of colleagues.

So I was feeling pretty cocky when the president came up to me at the Christmas party and complimented me once again on the Belfast shoot and the work I had been doing. About a half-hour later my sanity departed. I walked up behind the president and goosed him. He turned, looked at me, smiled, and said, "Oh Scully, I figured it had to be you."

I scurried away and hid behind my friends, chuckling like a high-school student.

And if that wasn't bad enough, I did the same thing fifteen minutes later, and then once more, this time with a huge palm leaf. At that point my friends and colleagues grabbed me, took me out to the parking lot, and put me in a cab.

Apparently, the president was going to fire me flat-out the next day, but my boss and a few colleagues talked him out of it. I apologized, explaining to him that I had been drunk. After a few days, pretty well everything was forgotten, but not surprisingly, many of my colleagues started to wonder even more about my connection to reality. Of course, I did too, but the problem was that I didn't really give a shit at the time. The president did, however, and he didn't turn his back on me for the rest of the time I worked at Global.

After four years at Global, I moved on and got a job working for CTV's *W-5*, a position that involved much more travel. From there, I went to CBC *Newsmagazine* — more travelling. And finally, I joined the much-respected CBC program *The Journal* — too much travelling.

On location in Hong Kong, April 1990.

I started seeing a "shrink," but it was no big deal. I was anxious and this guy was supposed to help. I was also a little depressed, but at that time I didn't understand how anxiety and depression were inextricably linked. It certainly all surfaced when I was sent to film a documentary in Hong Kong about the boat people who were still living in camps there after ten years. We had to get the buy-in of *National*

News for budgetary reason. At a meeting between the network's flag-ship national news team and us, I was asked what I thought. When everyone turned and looked at me, I panicked and haltingly opined: "It's a good story and we can do it."

They all waited for me to finish. But I had finished. I couldn't talk anymore in public. Later, I was told they were all pissed off at what they thought was my dismissiveness and arrogance. In the end, the docu-mentary went ahead and was a success. We won an international award for it as well as for a number of others I produced around the same time. Because my worldwide documentaries were applauded as con-sistently challenging, controversial, courageous, and well-made (that's a direct quote from a letter of recommendation I wrote to me, which I cunningly signed "Her Gracious Majesty, the Queen"), I was promoted to senior field producer at CBC's *The Journal* and given the first choice for any foreign shoot.

I went all over the world. One year I was away for nine months. It wasn't long until I was at my breaking point.

12

THE WEIGHT OF THE WORLD

As the song says, I've been everywhere, man. More than seventy countries — full-scale wars, civil wars, famine, all the horrors this world can offer, even sand-savaged Timbuktu. I went to Beirut thirteen times during the eight-year civil war, really pushing my luck. Those were bad times.

But the worst, the most deadly and sinister war I have ever covered, was Bosnia. From the surrounding hills, Serb snipers and heavy weaponry encircled the city of Sarajevo — and they shot on sight. Once, we saw four bodies lying in a river we passed every day; they were still there ten days later.

Car accidents were almost as deadly killers as the guns. It was murderous to drive down the main streets. Cars would blindly roar down the boulevards at up to two hundred kilometres an hour if they could, not looking left or right, but trying to scream to safety before the snipers got them. We did the same. The cameraman drove and I was his cross-street lookout. "Clear! Go! Go!" It was so dangerous that we only went out for two hours in the morning and two hours in the afternoon. That way we figured we had a better chance of not being killed.

One morning we were filming at a casualty aid station. Ambulances raced the wounded there first, and the doctors and nurses rushed to the door every time one pulled up under a small canopy. But the ambulance bay was in direct line of snipers in the nearby hills, and their aim was deadly. Some of them had apparently been on the Olympic team. That morning, they had already killed several of the Samaritans, nurses, and ambulance aides directly in their sights under the small green canopy. Aid stations were a great source of cash — the Serb high command was said to be paying US$600 for a dead doctor, $500 for a dead nurse, and about the same for a dead foreign journalist.

But it was the local media that was hit hard and brutally. Sixty had already died. The total number of civilians massacred by both sides has been estimated at up to 200,000, plunging humanity into degradation and evil not seen since the Nazis: The price for being a Serb civilian? Death. A Bosnian Muslim? Death. A Catholic Croatian? Death.

The murderous Serbs trumpeted their grotesque achievements the most. For once, I hope there is a higher power, only so those killers on all sides can answer to it and receive a bit more ferocious punishment than can be imposed by an international war crimes court.

One day, a boy about five years old was brought in to the aid station bleeding heavily from shrapnel wounds. An old woman who had just been hit by a bullet lay on a stretcher nearby. Other wounded — some badly shot — waited for their turn for triage, while their relatives wailed and moaned. The snipers were having a busy morning.

We were just about to leave the aid station when a Bosnian militiaman staggered in. He was in uniform. A black beret was jauntily sitting on the side of his head, a pistol in his belt. He appeared to be drunk, or high on drugs, and he was cradling a double-barrelled shotgun. I saw him the moment he swaggered through the door and wondered what the hell he wanted. He strolled directly over to me, with a wry smile of conquest on his lips. Suddenly, his face froze; he rammed the shotgun into my stomach and pulled the trigger. It wasn't loaded, or at least it didn't go off.

"A joke, my friend. A joke," he said.

Another time, in another part of the world, an aide to Yasser Arafat pulled a pistol on me. The Israelis had finally driven the Palestinian militias out of Beirut and into Syria. Arafat had left days before, but a few of his Fatah lieutenants had stayed behind to clear out the chairman's office and destroy any incriminating or classified papers. They built a bonfire in the street outside the office in West Beirut and set ablaze a pile of papers and posters. We filmed this symbolic end of the Palestinians as a force in Beirut and the cameraman handed me the tape as he reloaded his camera. Just then, one of Arafat's men, a guy I had come to know quite well over my many visits to the building, stormed up to me. "You have taken a picture of the chairman's face burning in the fire."

We hadn't, because there wasn't a picture of Arafat to be seen anywhere, much to my disappointment.

"No we haven't. There are no pictures of the chairman on the fire," I told him.

"That is not true. One of my men saw you take a picture of the chairman. Hand over the tape please, Mr. John."

"Like I said, we did not take any pictures of the chairman because there weren't any."

"I want the tape."

"I'm sorry. I'm not going to give it to you."

That's when he pulled out the gun and pointed it at me.

"Give me the tape."

A sane person would have complied, but I was so pissed off at this swaggering bully who thought he could control what went on television, I went nuts.

"I told you, we don't have any pictures of the chairman. Now put the gun away!"

He lowered it, but kept it pointed at me.

"Please, Mr. John, give me the tape."

"You are not getting it, but I'll make a deal. Let's go back to the hotel. We can screen the segment of the fire; if there's a picture of the chairman, you can have the tape. Deal?"

"Okay."

"But that's all I'm going to show you. That one segment. Deal?"

"Okay."

He kept the gun on his lap as we drove the twenty minutes back to the hotel. I kept the tape firmly clenched in my hands. At the hotel, I turned on the screening machine, fast-forwarded to the fire incident, and let the tape roll. No pictures of a flaming Arafat.

"See. I told you we didn't take any pictures of the chairman."

"Show me the rest of the tape, now."

"What? We had a deal. The deal was I would show you the part with the fire. Nothing else. Okay?"

"I want to see the rest of the tape."

"We made a deal. I trusted you to stick by your word, and now you're telling me you can't be trusted?"

I got my way, and we parted, both wondering who the stupider person was.

In another gamble that paid off big time, I convinced a Russian business jet crew to enter forbidden air space, then bribe the folks in the control tower with about one thousand U.S. dollars to let us land at the secret nuclear base of Murmansk in the far, far north of that vast and surly land.

What could they do to us? I thought. Was I kidding? I'd just been shooting a sequence of huge mass graves from the Stalin era in a forest in Siberia. That would be my future if we were caught. *But the story was sensational, worth at least a couple of years in a Soviet slammer,* I thought.

But I'd been in Russian prisons before, filming, and I certainly didn't want to end up in one, with the massive overcrowding, rampant illnesses like TB, and terrible gruel. Poor, hapless prisoners simply disappeared into that inhumane neverland or waited years for their cases to be heard while they festered, and often died, in those hell-pits.

This is what raced through my mind as I got up at 4:00 a.m. the next day. Three Russian activists straight out of a black-and-white movie, wearing long coats and hats pulled well down, were about to take us on a perilous trip. They wanted us to tape a scene the world did not know existed. It was dangerous. If we were caught, we'd probably be arrested as spies and the activists would disappear, never to be seen again.

John and a colleague aboard a chartered Russian jet en route to Murmansk, September 1992.

They wanted us to tape the Russian nuclear fleet. Not the submarines at sea, but eight or so rotting in the port of Murmansk, the ones constantly leaking radiation from their still-glowing reactors. The activists had a small motor-powered launch to ferry us out into the middle of the harbour so we could get better tracking shots and close-ups of the cancerous subs.

The dawn was grim and grey and the sea a menacing pewter. We started filming immediately in case we were caught, but no one appeared to notice us. Who would be crazy enough to land in Murmansk illegally, hire a boat, and in broad daylight actually tape their secret base? The emboldened activists then took us to the local hospital to see the results of those rotting underwater carcasses. On the way, I noticed gauges on street corners. There were two types. One gave the standard temperature reading; the other, that day's radiation levels.

The Murmansk Hospital was as bad as they get for dying cancer patients. But the doctors and nurses heroically allowed us into every corner of the facility, even if they, too, were taking huge risks. If they were caught letting a foreign TV crew take pictures of the suffering in

Murmansk, they would be jailed. But they wanted the world to know the dirty secret of their city.

There, I saw the dying and the nearly dead. I saw a three-year-old boy with all his fingers and thumbs bandaged with white gauze. His young mother explained to us that the gauze was there to try to stop her son from chewing off the tops of his fingers and thumbs when the pain of his cancer became unbearable.

We flew out of Murmansk undetected, or at least the bribe for the control tower had been spread around and everybody was happy.

Except the little boy who chewed the tops off his fingers.

Please forgive me for telling you one more episode about me on the road, but I am a journalist after all.

I call it the Rio Coco flu. It began with an exotic boat ride — two days in a flat-bottom boat, puttering down the mighty Rio Coco, which divides Costa Rica and Nicaragua. Six of us were headed for the camp of a Nicaraguan rebel leader, Commandant Zero, whose real name was Edén Pastora.

We stopped that first night on the riverbank and climbed up until we reached a tin shack that served as a restaurant. As usual, the meal was chicken and rice. At least I think that's what it was; we were eating by the light of a tiny candle, so I really had no idea what the bent old lady served us.

The next day we arrived at Pastora's camp, but he wasn't there. We filmed some of his rebels training, then headed back up the Rio Coco.

Two weeks later, I was back home when I received a phone call from a reporter from the *New York Times*. She asked if I had anything to do with the assassination attempt on Pastora. It had happened about a week earlier, when a press conference given by Pastora was ambushed by gunmen and grenade throwers. Pastora had survived; others hadn't.

"John, the Costa Rican paper *La Republica* did a two-page investigation into the ambush and they say you did it," she told me. "You were seen loading silver boxes onto a plane [true]. They could be full of arms and ammunition. They published the receipt for the plane with your name, full address, and home phone number."

"*They what?*"

"Yeah, I know. Outrageous. So where were you when the ambush took place?"

"I was back in Toronto. We all were."

The CBC urged my family and me to go into hiding, but I decided that these were just scare tactics. CBC crews and I were constantly in Central America giving reports that were often critical of U.S. policy in the region. Our documentaries, reported by Linden MacIntyre and Ann Medina, were shown on PBS in the United States, so many American politicians saw them and got pissed off, especially Ambassador Jean Kirkpatrick. True or not, I'm told she gave instructions for the CBC to be kept out of the region. Stupid woman; as if she could keep a Canadian crew out of anywhere.

Still, it all added to the pressure, the stress. About six months later, the whole thing a distant memory, I was coming back from a weekend at a rented cottage with Toni. I started to feel sick, a bit queasy. With incredible speed, the discomfort turned into a body-bending pain on my right side. At one point, Toni had to change a flat tire; I couldn't even lift it. As I became bent farther over with this terrible pain, we decided to head straight for Sunnybrook Hospital. As soon as we arrived, I was rushed into Special Care, where the doctors tried to figure out what was wrong. At first they thought it was a blood clot, so they gave me blood-thinners for several days. But I was getting worse. They told Toni two things: they might have to cut off the nerves in my side to ease the pain; and I was very ill and she should be prepared for my death.

A young intern suggested it could be something I picked up in Nicaragua.

"Don't be stupid," responded God, the senior doctor.

After a week, they switched medications, upped the morphine dose, and hoped. I'd worn a path to ultrasound, but in none of the five examinations did they find anything. Lucky for me I had a pushy GP who didn't buy this "we don't know" business. "Let me see the images," she snapped. Something had caught her eye.

"I want a biopsy done here. And please do it now. This man is very ill."

Uganda, 1984. John travelled to some of the most volatile countries in the world in his pursuit of the story.

In went the needle; out squirted a river of pus. It turned out I had an amoebic liver abscess, likely contracted from eating uncooked chicken.

So why did I do this for a living? Once I got going in television news and current affairs, I couldn't stop. Also, no law school or school of medicine would accept me. And, as you are probably gathering, I was addicted to it. Remember that syndrome psychiatrists call counterphobia, the compulsion to return to situations that terrify you because you love the challenge? That applied to me. The frenzy of travel and making documentaries in some of the remotest places on Earth buried my depression under a blanket of stress, excitement, danger, and achievement.

It was after covering all this shit that I made a crucial decision. I decided to return to New Zealand after being offered the job as head of TV New Zealand's current affairs department.

13

GOING HOME

The big Air New Zealand 747 with its silvery albatross wings banked over the astonishingly blue southern Pacific Ocean as it hung a left to put it on course for Auckland. The tail of the Boeing was emblazoned with the proud Maori Koru, an insignia that symbolizes strength and peace. And that's the kind of guy the captain was — relaxed and reassuring.

"Gidday, ladies and gentlemen, boy and girls. This is Captain Don Rutledge speaking. Hope you had a good night's sleep. That sure is a long trip. Ten hours and twenty-one minutes so far. Sorry to wake you, but we're just about in Auckland. Don't worry, there's still plenty of time for breakfast. We should be on the ground in exactly one hour's time. For connections, check the screen near the front. If you have any questions, please ask a member of the crew. Enjoy the rest of the flight. Thank you for flying Air New Zealand. *Kia Ora.*"

My first hint of the language of the indigenous Maori people. *Kia*

Ora: Hullo, how are you? I felt a little lump in my throat. I was coming home to a new job. I was going to be a heavyweight in New Zealand, the head of TV current affairs for the New Zealand Television Network, TVNZ. I had never been in charge of more than seven people at a time and now I was taking on a huge department (by Kiwi standards).

"What'll you have, mate?"

I was at the staff bar in TVNZ, near Wellington.

"Ooh, what do I want? A pint of Stella, please. No Stella? You got Steiney? Okay, two pints of Steinlager."

"Hey, John, I've bought you a welcome home drink. Here, I've opened it, already."

"Champagne! Kiwi Champagne! Wow, thanks."

It went in seconds, followed by more beer and a few chasers on the side. Drinking was a habit I would nurture even more in New Zealand.

Around this time, I found that I was unable to sleep, so I would anaesthetize myself with booze and collapse for about three hours. My brain whirred and chattered and swooped and dived and emerged from the period of supposed rest into a state of panic, fear, and intense agitation. And did I mention exhaustion?

So let me give you an idea of depression quickly building and asthma choking my lungs. Let me tell you about my first two days as TVNZ's head of current affairs.

I decided that one of my smart opening moves would be to visit all the news directors in the country. First on my list, through pure logistics, was Christchurch. To catch the plane, I had to get up at 6:00 a.m. and be at the airport by 7:30. At the end of the flight, the taxi dropped me at TNVZ Christchurch. It was 9:15.

"Hello, Rick. I don't think we've met before. I'm John Scully. I know I'm a bit early for the meeting, but as it's just you and me, we can get started, okay?"

"Sorry, John, I didn't get a chance to tell you …"

And that was just the beginning of the most perfect nightmare you could wish upon your greatest enemy.

"… I've got a dentist's appointment at 10:00 a.m. So I have to go," he finished, practically running out of the office. Not even a good-bye.

A news director? My second day! *Fuck me, you appalling prick,* I thought. I got the plane back to Wellington and wondered why I felt morose and sad.

My next disappointment was with the quality of the journalism at TVNZ. The network had a system of official complaints that was chaired by senior executives. The following issue left me speechless, perplexed, and outraged.

A hustling researcher had come across an important government document with whiteout across the secretive phrases. The researcher wiped the whiteout off and, presto, the government secret was revealed! Except the government claimed this was an unfair practice. You've got be kidding me. The two nozzles who made up the complaints committee sided with the government. They refused to accept my argument that what they denied was the very thing that we as journalists do. We uncover. In fact, the word *investigare* is Latin for peeling off, uncovering. And these two assholes were so gutless they had no idea of the ethics of journalism. I was told to get lost. I couldn't believe it.

The next disappointment pushed me closer to the edge. I formed a cut-and-run "instant" current affairs program, *The Cutting Edge.* Our first one-hour documentary was going to be a scorcher. Yachting's America's Cup was being sailed off the coast of Perth, Australia, and the network had cleared its schedule for this live, never-been-seen-before coverage of the race. The publicity and the costs were heavy, but the standard helicopter overhead coverage was brilliant. What I didn't know at the time was that the TV crew was incompetent. I proposed an instant doc and everyone agreed. We were due to take in a satellite feed of the race at 6:00 p.m. for replay an hour later, at 7:00 — just in case.

Early that evening, the phone rang. It was Mark, the senior producer, calling from Wellington. "John … it's all looking good. They're running a bit behind, but assure me they'll make the feed point in plenty of time."

At 6:30, he called back: "John, Mark. Bad news, mate. They're not going to make it!"

"Mark! Mark! Go live! We'll have to go live!"

"It's no use, John, they're still editing and they're an hour from the feed point."

"Jesus Christ, Mark, you never miss a deadline. Never! Did they lie?"

And so an historic first in the sordid history of TVNZ — the network went to black for half an hour. And I got the blame. I was overwhelmed with more thoughts of disbelief and utter sadness. They made us run the doc, the tape now physically back in Wellington, on Wednesday. It all went splendidly. No problems whatsoever. Apart from one fact: It was one of the biggest pieces of mindless shit to have been on the network in years.

I had come to New Zealand on my own. Toni and Emma wouldn't join me until several months later. My son, Jerome, didn't want to come back, so he returned to London, where he was born. So for those first few months, I had only my aging mom to talk to, and no one else. It was a worst case scenario.

Tears seeped out of my eyes and poured down my face with the slightest provocation, be it in public, in private, anywhere. I was alone … and I was cracking.

I found it impossible to comprehend leaks to newspapers that I was going to cut staff — I wasn't, but I was eventually ordered to because the others didn't have the guts.

I lived for television journalism, and my drive was so strong that I had utterly buried my depression for decades. But this repression only lasted as long as I had a job. At that point I knew I needed to see a psychiatrist or get some kind of help. I got a shrink instead. What's the difference between a shrink and a psychiatrist, you ask? None. Just my preference. I use "shrink" as a pejorative.

"Ah, Mr. Scully, how are you? Did you bring the cheque for the last visit?"

"I have it right here, doctor."

"Thank you, John. So what's going on? Nice socks, by the way. I'll bet you didn't get them here."

"Socks? I got them in Canada. Actually, I wanted to talk to you about my sleeping problems. I'm still having terrible troubles."

"Sleep problems? What are you on now?"

"Ten Rohypnols."

"Not working at ten, huh? Well, let's hit this thing on the head. Let's push the level up to fourteen."

"Is that a safe level, doctor?"

"I don't know. I'll ask my friend the chemist and tell you what he says when you come back next week."

One week later: "Mr. Scully! Cheque? I thank you. Now I heard back from my chemist friend. Funny thing. He says you're on a toxic dose of Rohypnol. So you'd better stop right away."

Yeah, right, stop right away. Stop yourself, asshole, especially when, surprise, surprise, I'd become addicted to the "roofies" that I had received courtesy of my own doctor.

Since I had returned to New Zealand, I had been seeing a lot of my mom, and she was very supportive. My father had been dead for ten years at this point, and because he hadn't been around to call the shots, she had become more confident. She noticed I was behaving a bit differently, and insisted on coming with me to talk to the doctor.

"Nothing's wrong with him, Mrs. Scully. By the way, I'm sorry about Ben. Great man."

"Well, there's something wrong, doctor."

"Nothing at all. All you need, Johnnie, is a bit more rest, some exercise, and maybe a day off or so. That'll work wonders. Seventy-nine dollars, please, John."

"Johnnie, this is not good enough," Mom told me after we left. "You're putting on an act when you go to see your doctor. He doesn't see the real you. I'm going back to tell him that he's killing you. He's addicting you and he's making your mental health much worse."

My mom on the warpath was a rare and wonderful sight. She'd take no shit from any second-rate shrink. She'd virtually nursed me for decades, and she wasn't going to let this guy kill me.

"Drop the dosage, doctor. Drop it today."

"Well, if that's what you and John want."

"It is what we both want," said Mom, fuming at this imbecile.
He dropped the dosage.

The "few beers" I had with my friend the night before the big meeting
must have been approaching a dozen by the way I felt the next morning.
I was so sick from the combination of booze and drugs, I could barely
move. The world according to John consisted of fog, echoes, and nause-
ating swing bridges.

The night before I had confided in one friend that a colleague said
I might be suffering from something like depression. Her reaction had
been, "What've *you* got to be depressed about?" It was the first time of
many that a friend would display ignorance about my disease.

That morning, I picked up the phone, slurred for a taxi, and managed
to get dressed in a neat shirt and tie. Tie! Me, wearing a tie? That should
have been a clue I was falling into the pit of mediocrity and conformity
from which there seemed to be no escape. Not that morning.

I had to take a one-hour flight from Wellington to Auckland for
the meeting, which was being held at the headquarters of the mighty
machine that was TV New Zealand.

It was one of those conference rooms I've endured a million times,
and a million times my heart has plunged — it was drab, utilitarian,
bare, harsh, defensive, and interfering, imposing its grey doom over this
TVNZ version of a séance. Around the table sat the cream of TVNZ,
although much of it had gone sour.

The boss began, imperiously.

"John, let's start with you. Could I have your budget projections for
next year?" he demanded.

"Budget projections? I thought this meeting was about staff cuts."

"Listen to me, old darlin'." He spat out the bullying words as I cow-
ered at one end of the table. "Get it right, will you? And get me that
budget now!"

I had no fight, just cowardice, humiliation, and despair. How could I
have screwed that up? *Oh, God, I feel terrible. Stupid.*

"I'll have to call Wellington and—"

"I don't care what you have to do. Just do your job properly and get the budget."

"Yes, sir."

After a quick phone call, I retrieved the sacred papers from the fax machine in the adjacent office, but as I turned to return to the abuse and ridicule, my already scrambled head started to swim a little harder. The dizziness made its way to my wobbling legs and my speech became slurred. I was semi-conscious, staggering. I had to sit down.

"John! Are you all right?"

The boss was showing unusual compassion.

Bang! My head crashed down on the table as I passed out momentarily.

At that point, I had to come clean. I told my boss and his boss, truthfully, that I was on multiple medications, including anti-anxiety drugs, and they were all giving me awful side effects. And I admitted I was addicted to two of them, lorazepam and Rohypnol. Again, the boss showed unusual sympathy by finding me a mental institution and also picking up the tab. Still, he helped *drive* me crazy, so I guess it was only right.

The very next day I was on a plane bound for Dunedin. Once we landed, I hired a cab, which took me down a long country road; there was no sign of the city as we drove. We slowed as we approached a high fence draped in trees and I saw a wide, sweeping driveway that led up to the hospital, Ashburn Hall.

A nurse greeted us at the door. "Ah, Mr. Scully, we've been expecting you. Now I just need you to fill out some forms, then I'll take you to your room. The doctor has slotted you in for three o'clock."

When the nurse came back, I was frightened and convinced I would never heal from whatever I had in my head. I started to have a panic attack. "How long will I be here?" I asked.

"Perhaps two months. You've a very serious addiction problem."

"Two months! I don't have two months."

I felt the shuddering, convulsive pitching and yawing of tears of pain and panic. *I'll lose my job!* I thought. My sobbing and gut-wrenching agony left no doubt that I had lost control. I had stopped thinking, stopped talking properly, instead blurting out a drug-twisted patois.

The headline read "TVNZ Boss in Mental Hospital."

Who the fuck would care? I thought.

As it turned out, most of the country, apparently. New Zealand is a small country, with a population of just four million at that time, and I felt that every single one of them had read the story that I was hospitalized in a place they all called the "loony bin."

There are hundreds of regular psych wings of hospitals and specialized institutions around the world, but none could approach Ashburn Hall, either in cost, efficacy, or its dubious location. Ashburn Hall is a massive old manor house that hangs in the foothills on the outskirts of a bleak, dark city called Dunedin, whose most famous annual event was once stated, I reckon in a spoof entry, in Wikipedia as "nude rugby." Dunedin's 125,000 suburban robots shiver on the lower east coast of the South Island. Dunedin was, is, and always will be an old Scottish Presbyterian city with a university renowned for its medical faculty, not its psychiatric faculty.

I had fallen so far. From the head of the current affairs department of a country's TV network to the place they called the loony bin.

At Ashburn Hall, the biggest challenge for the staff was to find someone to help clean up after meals. I am not kidding. How do you persuade a patient to carry the food waste from funny farm to pig farm?

"You see, John, the patients do most of the housework, as well as the cleaning and cooking. Now, what have we given you to do? Do you peel potatoes, John?"

Instinctively, and as it would turn out stupidly, I blurted out, "No!" before I heard the other offers.

"No worries. I've got just the job for you."

So the head nurse had me, the patient, seven days a week, collecting the garbage cans of stench, pouring them into two large rusting buckets, braving Dunedin's bitter, wet, misty mornings, and trudging maybe five minutes across soggy hillocks until I reached the porkers. First one bucket of sludge oozed, bumped, trickled, and cascaded into a large chest-high barrel, then the other. Pig slop à la carte. What a brilliant idea.

The facility housed about twenty patients (I refuse to use the nonsensical, politically more correct term *clients* and its implication of business not healing.) Down the hill, a short distance away, was the building where old folks went to die. What both groups had in common was my *bête noir*: food. But there's no point in complaining about hospital food — it's the same everywhere. Not good, but not nearly as foul as we all pretend. After each meal, appetizing or not, the patients scraped their half-empty food plates into garbage cans. Porridge slopped over bacon swimming in a mixture of orange juice, toast, runny fried eggs, floods of milk, goops of gravy, brown-going-on-blue beef, very used tissues, tea bags, dozens of ash-filled plastic coffee cups, the odd banana skin, if one was lucky, and a projection of vomit and other detritus that delighted the farmer's dozen grunters.

The farmer loved it. Ashburn Hall loved it. All they had to do was wait for the next fall guy. Sorry, I mean the next poor sufferer who came there to heal.

Big, brooding, red-cheeked Andy was the only guy at Ashburn who volunteered to peel the morning buckets of potatoes. Andy was around thirty, overweight, unmarried, unemployed, penniless, and, I guess, profoundly depressed and too alone for any human being. His family, as in most cases, paid the freight. He told me over and over that when he left hospital he would go to his "crib" or cottage in the wilderness of a province called Southland. This was going to be his place of respite and recovery. Poor bastard. He was very sick and could barely speak. Shovelfuls of meds had done that to him. So the combination of Andy and the lonesome crib pointed in one terrible direction. But I reckon it was inevitable. He was going to be released in a week or so to make room for even sicker patients. Sicker than Andy? I guess I was lucky to get in a month earlier. Maybe someone pulled some strings.

There was another guy I unkindly nicknamed "The Axe Murderer." He had been one year short of finishing his degree when he had cracked under the stress. His eyes had become glaring and enraged. He wasn't really a killer. He didn't even throw a punch. A miniscule number of mentally ill patients are violent, and often it's because of a combination of medication, booze, and street drugs, or because they go off their prescribed medication. But I think the Axe Murderer was hit by severe depression, choking anxiety, and, most importantly in this case, he'd lost his short-term memory, focus, and concentration.

I also met Phyllis, who hadn't been able to sleep properly for two decades. She described how half a dozen times every night she would awake with a bang, gasping.

Catherine was perpetually dressed in black. She had a pretty alabaster face and long, lovely brunette hair. But Catherine was in such severe psychosis she refused to leave the hospital, or even to engage in any group discussions or games. She'd been at Ashburn Hall for seven months. Ugh.

And then there was "Rat Man." I hate to use the word, but he was well and truly nuts. I first became aware of him at the daily morning meeting. There, the dozen patients who turned up put their chairs in a circle and waited for the nurse.

One day, after the nurse arrived, the meeting got underway.

"Good morning, everyone. Why don't we start this morning with a round of feelings?"

"My name is Phyllis. This is my fifth week and I feel like two out of ten."

"My name is Dennis. (The trainee axe murderer) This is my third week. I'm about a four."

"My name is Ray and I want to bring up the matter of my pet rat."

He wasn't kidding.

"He's lovely and friendly. Look."

The group recoiled en masse as Ray pulled "Sir Winston" out from under his sweater. The creature was pink, smooth-skinned, and the size of a piglet.

"And since there's a pet cat here, what's the difference in having a pet rat?" he asked. "They're clean. I'll keep it in my room. No one need ever see it."

The nurse procrastinated. How was she going to deal with this idiot?

The argument went on for ten minutes, but ended suddenly when the nurse announced emphatically, "I've decided. No rats will be allowed to be kept at Ashburn Hall."

"How are you feeling this morning, John?"

"Okay, thanks."

"Good. The doctor will see you now. He's the staff psychiatrist. Brilliant man. Brilliant. Come. I'll show you the way."

The psychiatrist I was led in to see was a Scot nearing retirement age. He had grey hair and a neatly trimmed beard. His office was tiny and flooded with books and magazines.

That first time I met him he said, "Mr. Scully, I've read your file, and I have a number of comments."

He was professional, kindly, and competent.

"What you've got to do is get plenty of sleep and plenty of exercise. One of the best cures for depression and addiction is vigorous exercise."

Depression? This was the very first time it had been officially diagnosed, in passing. I was fifty.

"When would I take the exercise, doctor?"

"Any time, Mr. Scully. Why not now, before dinner?"

I took the doctor at his word, put on a jacket, and turned headlong into an Antarctic wind that screamed up the road. *Walk! Walk! Faster, you idiot,* I told myself.

The doctor said to get plenty of exercise, but God, it was cold! Then my asthma kicked in and started to choke me. I couldn't breathe.

Not again!

"Mr. Scully, you must take things easier. Now, here, take this inhaler."

The headline of my life: "Just Take It Easier."

Yeah, nothing like an asthma attack on the second night in my first psychiatric institution.

Some people used to call me "the chemist," or "Dr. John," because of the rainbow of medications I carried with me to every corner of the globe. I had stuff to put you to sleep for a week, or keep you up for just as long, some neat painkillers, and a hidden pouch with prescription narcotics. All wonderful junk for the body, of course, but what about the brain? Nobody ever worried about the brain.

Speaking of the brain, I'll try to explain the way I thought back at Ashburn Hall, where I used what I call my "white wall" for the first time.

My white wall, my only ally, encased and hid me in a cape of desperate vacuity. I could talk to it, and it would talk back. The wall was my escape from depression into another, much wackier world, where it not only talked back, but gave me cheek. I even used it to access one of the greatest brains in history — apart from mine — Albert Einstein's:

Ah, the human brain, meant to weigh about three pounds; mine, well most of the time it feels like a meek, atrophied few ounces. By comparison, Al Einstein's grey engine chugged in at a sleek 2.71 pounds. But when he had a great idea, Mr. E's brain allegedly ballooned to a stunning 3.5 pounds. That's when he got his E=mc² eureka moment.

What did it mean? Al felt sure he had stumbled upon his greatest solution to the world's daily problems. E=mc²: Everyone (wants) = two Big Macs! And if in some benighted country they could only afford one burger, the theory, relatively, remained constant. So Uncle Al, the kiddies' pal, officially entitled it The Theory of Relatives. So my wall called Al. I told you I was thinking a bit strangely. But of course I projected that it was Al who really had the problem.

"Al, baby. Have you lost your mind again? Gone off the old meds, have we?"

"No, no. It's just that I feel so inspired. I can change the world. So what do you want?"

"Your new theory? I think its bullshit."

"Oh, dear boy, it is. I was on Paxil when I wrote it."

"Paxil?"

"Yes. It came to me after downing fifteen milligrams of Imovane, as a sleeper, and the Paxil, and I thought 'I'll just make up some rubbish to go with it to confuse mathematicians for decades.'"

But Al had enough chatting to me through my wall for the day and said goodbye.

After a couple of years, I left Al Einstein and his wall and the poison of TVNZ and tried out for a job with the fledgling New Zealand network TV3. I was fired from there after just six months. I agreed with the job termination.

Next, I was close to being given a job as a field producer at another Australian network. When they sent over a crew to test me out, it was as though I'd never been near a television set or camera, let alone practiced journalism. I couldn't do the most basic chore, such as listing the shots on videotape. My speech was even worse, almost incomprehensible with drug-induced slurring. No one could make any sense of what I was saying, and the exasperated reporter unloaded on me big time. I knew right away I wasn't getting the job.

While the depression had been officially diagnosed, which was a big help, I had regressed badly. And it would be two more decades before my current psychiatrist diagnosed post-traumatic stress disorder (PTSD) … both from childhood and from my experiences as an adult.

"Go back to Canada, John. This place will kill you."

That was the smartest advice I ever received. It came from one of the few good psychiatrists I've ever met. I started seeing him after my Ashburn Hall sojourn. Not only was he a New Zealand senior health official, but he made time, his time, to call me every day to see how I was doing. He tried very carefully to alter my meds and doses. He was humble, generous, and very much in tune with his patients. What a rarity. But he, too, moved on, in his case to Australia. But not before a few kind words of farewell:

"John, do you have my cheque?"

14

BACK TO CANADA

I took my doctor's advice and flew back to Canada with my family in 1987. I got a job with the prestigious CBC investigative program *The Fifth Estate*, but for reasons which are still unclear to me, the reporter I was working with, already a household name, treated me like dog crap. I guess he thought I was carving out his precious territory; maybe he didn't like my driven personality. Regardless, his attitude did wonders for my depression.

My first assignment was a very difficult investigative story on immigrants who were buying their way into Canada. I needed a whistleblower, but was getting nowhere. I was also so stricken with anxiety that I was unable to answer the phone — not a good state for an investigative journalist to be in.

The executive producer eventually started needling me to deliver. She had a point, but I'd just courageously (for me) spoken to a great whistleblower and he was still deciding whether to appear on camera or not.

"John, I need this story for next week," she insisted.

"I'm sorry, but I'll need just one more week. I've almost got it," I told her.

But she was having none of it.

"No, John. For next week."

I panicked, and the anxiety and depression kicked in. In my unbalanced state, I dashed off a letter of resignation. In it I said I was "totally inadequate for the job" and "too far out of my depth." A healthy John would never have allowed a situation like this get so far out of hand and would have sailed through this item. But this new intense stress, plus tension, depression, anxiety, and an utterly remorseful demeanour that had taken me over, battered me into a sort of "brain freeze." I was so severely mentally distressed that I was unable to think straight. I thought no one in the universe could help me. I was so disgusted with myself. I would often leave the *Fifth Estate* office and walk down to city hall, where I would sit in the square and seethe and weep. *I was a loser. Useless. I'd never be a journalist again.*

The boss read my resignation through twice, put it down, and, to my surprise, said "Yes. I think that's best. You can leave today."

That's typical of folks like us. In states of depression, our judgment, equilibrium, balance, and sound mind desert us, and we do things that are way out of character. In that list of signs of depression they left off a critical one: tears. Sudden, unexplained crying is often a screaming indicator of depression.

That's what happened a week after I accepted my next job with CBC Toronto. On my first day, I was nervous, monosyllabic, frightened, and hesitant. They gave me a desk and disappeared. I did the crossword while waiting for an assignment or an introductory meeting. After about an hour, the deputy editor came up to me.

"John, could the boss and I see you in his office?"

"John, we didn't hire you to do crosswords. We'd like some work out of you, please."

I walked out of the newsroom, again stunned, and met Toni for lunch at a nearby mall. As I started to tell her what happened, I burst into tears. Not just a few drops, but waterfalls of howling public pain. People looked away in embarrassment, but I didn't care where I was. I was grieving, grieving so passionately for the loss of my skills and the lack of understanding of my bosses. The crying lasted half an hour.

I went back to the CBC that afternoon, and over the course of two years managed to claw my way back to professionalism, despite the fact that I was experiencing breath-defying panic attacks during the daily meetings. The symptoms were frightening and embarrassing. It got to the point where I didn't dare to talk at all.

Panic attacks can be ameliorated with drugs and therapy. When they happen, you actually panic, thinking catastrophic thoughts of a heart attack, stroke, immediate death, loss of mental control, and, for me, this strange loss of breath and inability to speak. The good news is that no one dies of a panic attack, but the frustration and the alliance with depression are not a good mix. *They* can kill you.

In 1993, after the kids had left home, I decided to take one more crack at covering news abroad when I was posted to the new New Delhi bureau in India. Toni and I had been there only one year when I received a call from the boss.

"Hello, John? Toronto calling. How are you doing over there?"

"Fine, thanks."

Oh, damn, I thought. It was the head of news and current affairs calling, and she only called when the shit was hitting her fan. She was, when at her best, charming, but I did not respect her lack of journalistic expertise. Still, she was the boss, and this was the first time I had heard from her since we had set up the bureau.

"John, I've got some bad news, I'm afraid. We're closing New Delhi and Mexico City. The budget cuts just won't sustain them."

"What? When does this happen?" I asked.

"We'd like you to start packing now and come back to Toronto."

"And what will I do there?"

"We haven't figured that one out yet."

"Do you have a job for me?"

"Well, actually, John, not at the moment. I've got HR looking."

This was not just bad news; it was a slap in the face.

"So there's no job for me?" I pressed.

"Not at the moment. And by the way, you're on contract, not staff, so we are not bound to accommodate you any further."

"How do you mean?"

"We'll do our best to find you work, but I can't guarantee … hold on please, John. That's my other line, and I think it is HR.

"Ah, huh. Yes. And when would the job start, because he's in India at the moment? I see. That's fine then. John will be thrilled."

Thrilled? Had they found me a chance to do my own documentary series? To head up the investigative unit? Things might be turning around.

"John, I've just spoken with HR and they've found a job writing scripts in the Windsor newsroom."

"You mean to tell me I have travelled the world and covered endless wars and risked my life for the CBC and this is what you offer me — a job in the Windsor newsroom?"

"Well, I'm afraid that's all there is. Take it or leave it. Oh, and could you please bring all the edit equipment back with you. So, can I say you'll move from Toronto to Windsor?"

"No you may not. I'm quitting," I told her emphatically.

"In that case, we require you to be out of your apartment within three days."

So I moved to back to Canada and started looking for work. I was by then in my early fifties, and even though I was one of the more qualified television journalists on the international stage, I couldn't get a job with anybody in India, London, or Toronto.

Ageism was truly alive, and the rejection slips poured in, literally by the dozen. I even called in a favour at the BBC with a former friend who was now hiring. In a pompous, formal, officious five-minute conversation, he said he would ask around and let me know. He must be incredibly thorough; twenty years later I still haven't heard back from him.

Sometime later, I was saved by two good Samaritans who thought I had been treated poorly, and I was offered a contract job training CBC journalists and upgrading their skills. Boy, did I need the money! But the position, once again, required me to do extensive travelling. So for the next three years, I crisscrossed the country, stopping at every place the CBC had a news service, from Yellowknife to Iqaluit (six times) to St. John's, and every town in between.

But all that relentless travel proved extremely stressful for me. Being back on the road and living out of hotel rooms became a big problem. Because I had stopped travelling with a crew, I found myself staying alone in hotels for weeks at a time. I would teach until 4:00 p.m., walk back to the hotel, have a few drinks, watch TV, eat dinner, take my meds, and go to bed. I no longer had a crew to carouse with after hours. I had a job, but it was destroying me.

Once, while I was training in Montreal, I was gulping down a new mixture of SSRIs (selective serotonin reuptake inhibitors) and anti-anxiety meds. I poured myself a very large rum and cola and turned on the television. Within fifteen minutes, I was completely paralyzed; I couldn't move. This terror lasted half an hour. When I was finally able to get up, I took a few steps toward the bed, tripped, and crashed dizzily across the bed frame. I lay there for ten minutes before trying to get up. God, my chest hurt. Not surprising, as I had cracked four ribs in the fall.

I repeated the same concoction the next night to see if it was an accident or a really serious problem. This time, my body and my brain froze after a mere five minutes and I couldn't move a muscle for an hour. I should have gone straight to the hospital, but I couldn't move.

I experienced a similar effect from the much-used anti-depressant bupropion. (This drug is also prescribed as a smoking "cure" under the brand name Zyban.) The bupropion caused me to have seizures and suffer paralysis without warning: I even collapsed in the street several times before I got off the drug.

During that time, Toni and I moved to Muskoka. The kids were grown and working, and Toni and I were broke. So we sold our home in Toronto and bought an inexpensive house in the woods near the little town of Dwight, Ontario. We were searching for financial relief and a more relaxed lifestyle, but the next few years turned out to be anything but relaxed, and the three-hour drive to the airport and all points beyond in Canada was tiring and stressful for me. Once again, the job was killing me. It was time to look for something else.

I applied for the position of senior producer at Vision TV in Toronto. The female exec of the station's current affairs program, *360 Vision*, tried valiantly to cover her astonishment at the interview when she discovered

I was not the Twinkie of twenty-five she was expecting but grumpy old me at the age of sixty.

"Why, you must be John," she said warmly, having completely recovered after getting up off the carpet. She interviewed me for half an hour. At a second meeting, she and I had coffee outdoors and she asked me the elephant in the room question: "John. How do you feel about working for a woman of my age?"

I replied, slightly more politely, that I couldn't give a shit. A boss was a boss.

I got the job.

Even though Toni and I had not been living up north in Dwight for long, I decided to get an apartment in Toronto to obviate the tedium, the fatigue, and the bumpy three-hundred-kilometre bus ride back and forth. We didn't have enough money, but I managed to wrangle some more from the company and paid some myself. But this arrangement meant that I now lived alone all week — again, not good for the depression. To compound things, on the day I started at Vision, a close friend was admitted to hospital with terminal cancer. It was an awful day. Soon after, I got the news that another close friend had killed himself. He was only twenty-four. There was no inquest; it was ruled just another suicide.

Living alone was not just a mental challenge. Having been up north in the woods for several years, I found myself blocking my ears to cut out the twenty-four-hour cacophony of sirens heading to the nearby hospitals. Most days I would shop for ready-to-eat cooked food on Toronto's main drag, Yonge Street (my cooking skills extend to boiling an egg and making a lovely cuppa tea).

I worked at Vision for three and a half years. Together, the exec and I raised the level of our current affairs program to something respectable. We were even nominated for a Gemini Award. But unfortunately the ratings were low, and the program was cancelled. Both the exec and I were let go.

During that time, I had been working on my first book, *Am I Dead Yet?* I also got to know my current psychiatrist. He was not just a psychiatrist, he was also a researcher and an associate professor at the University of Toronto — and refreshingly professional. It took about three years of visits before we warmed to each other, but he was the best psychiatrist I have ever had, and I am still seeing him.

A lot of my time during that period was consumed by juggling showers of multi-coloured mind machines with names like Prozac, mirtazapine, Zoloft, Effexor, Seroquel, Nardil, Cymbalta, and amitriptyline. Every day I took about twenty-five pills, most of them at night. If that wasn't enough, after one visit to a sleep clinic I was diagnosed with severe sleep apnea, the result of which is that I get almost no restful REM sleep. I found their sophisticated breathing machines suffocating, so they weren't much help.

One of the drugs the doctors at the clinic prescribed to help me sleep was called nabilone, or Cesamet. Nabilone contains, wait for it, horror of horrors, cannabis, so it's categorized as a "controlled substance." This makes it a huge pain to get from the pharmacy. Every single time I needed a refill, the folks at the drug store went into paroxysms of flailing confusion and doubt. It generally took a week's warning, three or four phone calls, and, nearly always, a personal visit to the pharmacy, carrying my empty pill bottles to prove I was out of them.

Then there was the fat-producing sleeper and anti-psychotic Seroquel. I put on twenty pounds while on the drug and it refused to come off, not an ounce of it. The ancient anti-depressant Nardil also helped the fattening follies. Add to that the clonazepam I took for anxiety and a dose of six gabapentin capsules, which were prescribed for my fibromyalgia.

For pain, I took oxycodone — the demon of the street — but god, did I get sick, as it reacted very badly with my other meds. When I was taking it, I would suddenly fall over or literally drop a full cup of tea that I forgot I was holding; maniacal states came and went; deep, brain-emptying depression. I finally gave up the oxys and switched to the safer but far less effective Tylenol 1s.

It's a common misconception that anti-depressant drugs make you high. The aim of drugs like Prozac (fluoxetine), first billed as the designer drug of the twentieth century, is to even out the mood, to lift it to where a normal person's mood is. But the side effects, like with many meds, can be brutal, and few of us are immune.

The list of drugs I've mentioned above is pretty typical therapy for depression and its associated symptoms, but the bottom line is that I still don't know what the drugs are doing to my mind or my body. It can't be good. A common long-term side effect of many of these drugs is memory loss. But loss of memory can be attributed not just to the drugs, but to the disease itself, which is scary. Conditions like dementia and Alzheimer's trip gaily across a dispirited brain. When you're taking a mixture of meds like me, it's difficult for doctors to figure out which drug may be causing the memory loss. If you're truly worried, I suggest you check with your local Alzheimer's Society.

The debate still rages about the efficacy of anti-depressants, the manipulation of the brain chemical serotonin, and the benefits of talk therapy, particularly Cognitive Behavior Therapy (CBT), which I'll explore in greater detail later in the book. It seems like there's a new, persuasive dissenting voice every week. All I can offer as guidance is to relate to you my experience, but I absolutely believe that if a particular therapy works for you, even if it's been shown to be a placebo or a fad, you should go for it. Science is so far away from finding a cure for depression that it's every sick brain for itself. One school posits that the SSRIs such as Prozac are very beneficial for folks with mild depression, but recently I came across another study that debunked this finding and averred that not only did the drug prompt suicidal thoughts, it was only effective for *serious* depression. Whom do you believe? I think, in the end, it comes down to you, with the guidance of a trusted mental health professional, to decide what's best for *your* mind, *your* mood, and *your* body.

15

BACK IN TREATMENT

It was going to be one the most memorable events in my life — the launching of my first book at a noted Toronto bookstore — yet it would end in disaster.

The book launch kept me preoccupied, which for me is usually a good thing; except, of course, I overdid it. One day I did two live television interviews, beginning with a full hour about me with a star CBC reporter, who afterward agreed with his producer that the interview was "inspiring." He also suggested it should be seen by "journalism students in the country." There was then another hour of the same magnificent subject on the Documentary Channel. Then there was radio, live and taped. In all, a dozen CBC radio stations interviewed me across the country that day. I had to do it. That's what the publicists wanted. And I was in full adrenalin mode.

In Guelph, two people showed up for my book launch speech; the crowds were better elsewhere. A week later, the big night finally arrived.

It started out very well, with many friends and close colleagues making an appearance along with a few other folks. I was coming to the end of my speech, about to hit the punch line, when a booming voice from the floor shouted, "If you carry on like this, we'll be here 'til midnight."

I balked for a fraction of a second, shocked and shaken, but managed to finish my speech and answer questions.

Guess who had interrupted me? Get this: the agent for my publisher. Open bars are a disaster! But instead of confronting him, I, an absolute neophyte in the publishing world, said nothing.

Despite my rage, I managed to thank the audience. But I was devastated.

As Toni and I walked up Toronto's Bay Street after the launch, looking for something to eat, *zip*, I suddenly had a depression crash. The stress was just too much.

"Is that it? Is that all there is?" I said to her.

I flashed back thirty years to Apollo. I was turning my evening of celebration into catastrophe. I could feel the tears welling up, the black despair plunging deeper than I could recall it ever going. I had stepped into what I describe as my own metaphoric private elevator shaft. Step down and die.

This phenomenon is common with us mentally ill folks. Once we have achieved a goal, we wonder why we bothered. The enjoyment is utterly momentary. I couldn't take it anymore, and I said to Toni, "I want to kill myself."

If she hadn't been there to stop me, I know I would have committed suicide that night.

I had one final engagement in Ottawa. From there, I called my psychiatrist, and a day later I was back in another fucking mental hospital.

The facility I entered was AIM, which stands for Alternate Inpatient Milieu. It is part of the Centre for Addiction and Mental Health's new, advanced method of treating in-patients.

The AIM units are located on White Squirrel Way in Toronto, in new buildings that look like low-rise apartments. Each patient is now given a private room and separate bathroom and shower with a door.

Compared with other wards I've been in, AIM was like a Holiday Inn without the mini-bar. One unit treats depression, bipolar disorder, and OCD; another treats general addictions. Many famous faces have passed through those doors, but I'm not allowed to say who.

The history of asylums around the world has been horrendous — howling, overcrowded madhouses. But CAMH is taking a revolutionary approach. It's in the middle of rebuilding the 150-year-old fortress on Toronto's Queen Street West, and the plan aims to integrate the facility with the local businesses. Construction is well underway as I write this, and when completed will include a shopping mall, housing, and pedestrian thoroughfares. CAMH swears all the local business people are 100 percent behind the scheme.

So from the darkest days of ridicule and stigma, at least there is hope, at least in Toronto. Apart from a seemingly scant sixty beds for patients, CAMH will operate what they call the Intergenerational Wellness Centre, which will combine the hospital's Child, Youth and Family Program with their Geriatric Mental Health Program. Along with the forty-eight beds for seniors with complex mental health issues, the centre will include Canada's first full-service twelve-bed inpatient program dedicated to youth struggling with both addiction and mental illness.

At least it's progress.

When I arrived at AIM that first time, the facility had just opened, and the new Alternate Milieu setting was still in chaos, with the computers failing to dispense the right medications and therapy delayed or postponed. An impatient patient hung around the dispensing office. A few feet outside the locked front door, I observed billows of smoke coming from cheap tobacco. Cigarettes are the only lifeline for many mentally ill folks, and it seems cruel to me to banish these people, especially those who are quite sick, to the outdoors.

A nurse took me to my room but, unlike the worst institutions (I have been in two of those), here no one searched my bags for knives, razors, scissors, or drugs — basically, anything I could kill myself or my neighbour with. AIM was instantly more calming and trusting, despite being filled with very sick people, though not nearly as sick as those in other wards. This facility was for folks ostensibly on the way back to sanity. The stay there is voluntary, and I was free to follow my own wishes if I wanted.

The facility offered decent meals and snacks, hockey was on the television, and the beds were adequate. Treatment continued off and on throughout the day. Some patients were locked in but those who had a pass from their doctor could leave on the weekend, as long as they were back by Sunday night.

During my stay, I usually remained in the hospital on weekends, but I was allowed to go for long walks most days. During the week, after breakfast, I'd pile on my coat and trek smartly over to Starbucks for a skull-bursting Colombian. Don't know what the docs would say about that. Actually, yes, I do: "Only in the morning. It'll ruin your sleep."

Each night between 10:00 p.m. and 7:00 a.m. the nurses made hourly checks on each patient to make sure there were no calamities, no suicides.

I have been to AIM a total of four times, and stayed for about six weeks each time. Before each visit, I had traumatic events. There were warning signs, but I couldn't stop myself from experiencing what they used to call a nervous breakdown.

During my stays at AIM, I attended many of the programs that were offered. One of these was quite different from the programs offered at other hospitals I'd been to. It was run by a recreational therapist, and in it I learned therapeutic breathing as a part of an array of training. I was encouraged to keep an active lifestyle, which I was told would help the depression. The therapists emphasized gentle stretching, Tai Chi, and yoga, which they claimed would improve my physical abilities and my mood, increase my socialization skills, and improve my routine by structuring my days. I was given handouts on the exercises so I could continue them once I was back at home.

Another part of this mental fitness program included visits to interesting city sites with the occupational therapist. The idea was to get us out, to see new things, and to meet new people.

One therapeutic breathing exercise still really works for me whenever I get obsessive thoughts. It focuses my mind on the rhythm of breathing, which helps me to eliminate stress. It is also supposed to support the physical body, transform overpowering emotions, and restore peace of mind. It takes a lot of work to achieve a good, flowing motion, but the payoff is worth it.

The first three times I was in a mental hospital, I was there primarily to be stabilized, and in the process hopefully get some relief from the depression. Afterward, I always felt better and less suicidal, but that's hardly living, is it? Avoiding suicide is a full-time job. Trying to lessen the pain of depression and anxiety will engulf you if you let it. In most hospitals I've been in, there's a lot of emphasis on therapeutic healing in addition to drug therapy.

Memorials don't mean much to me, except for one. This one is simple, some would say even crude, and it's hidden on a small Toronto street beside AIM. You can barely see it from the road. There's a brick wall there — my other wall. Not the one I gaze at in fits of boredom, but the remains of an encircling brick fortress that evokes the heroism and the horror of the inmates of the "asylum" that sat on Queen Street West in Toronto 150 years ago. The inmates themselves were ordered to build that wall to ensure they didn't escape — and to keep prying eyes from seeing what lay behind the towering, prison-like facade. The officials gave this practice of slave labour the appalling euphemism "Work Therapy Program."

Thankfully, the small part of the wall that's still standing is being preserved, even as the entire site is being rebuilt. The wall poignantly reminds me of the fight today to treat mental illness as you would any other medical issue — with dedicated concern — especially as scientists search for alternative treatments. The attitudes that staff and doctors have toward patients has changed dramatically over the years. For the most part, the units I've been in have treated me with respect and dignity, and they even listened to some of my inane suggestions. And I've never been asked to lift even one brick.

16

ON THE MOVE AGAIN

Bad news always seems to come in the middle of the night. Folks don't normally phone for a chat at 3:00 a.m., and the call from New Zealand jangled us all awake.

Toni answered the phone. It was her sister Tricia.

"Oh, thank god you're home," she said. "The news is not too good, I'm afraid. Mummy has slipped into a coma."

"How sick is she?" Toni asked.

"The doctor says he doesn't know how long she's got left. Not long, would be my guess."

Toni's mum was ninety-two, but up until that time had been bright and alert and living with a dozen or so seniors in a home run by nuns. But now she was dying. Toni had to decide whether to fork out for a gouging last-minute fare to New Zealand or stay at home and regret not taking the last chance to see her mum alive.

She decided to go.

Before she left for the month-long trip, I made Toni a promise that I would not commit suicide while she was gone. Not an easy deal, as I would be living on my own, isolated.

After she left, I was terrified to leave the house, and too panic-stricken to perform the most menial tasks. Once during that time, my kids, Emma and Jerome, drove the four hundred kilometres round-trip from the big city with a pile of food for me.

Every night that month, our friend Eva rang me to make sure I was okay. It was a lovely gesture of unfailing generosity. I lied once or twice and told her I had food. I didn't. Well, not much; I had stuff that had been in the cupboards and the fridge for weeks.

Intellectually, I used the wall for hours at a time. At about the start of week three, I felt a pain in my chest and tears began pouring down my cheeks. I was starting to crash very suddenly. It was time for emergency action.

I called my psychiatrist and told him I was coming apart and was suicidal. It was a Thursday night, so I left a voicemail. By the time the paperwork had been cleared it was Monday. I had already promised myself that I wouldn't go into any lockup ward or any unit that drove my depression through my skull. Lockups seldom helped my depression.

But then I remembered I had no one to take care of the house, the snow, or the two cats. Toni took care of that and got our neighbour Eva to help.

Three days after the call to my psychiatrist and a fitful, wasted, tear-drenched weekend, I hopped on a bus for the four-hour trip from Huntsville to Toronto. When I arrived, I took a taxi straight to CAMH on College Street. I broke down again within minutes of starting to talk to my psychiatrist. I had a no control over my emotions and I had lost all of my composure. I was shaking; I had given up hope. My psychiatrist thought I was so sick that he admitted me to the hospital to adjust my meds and get me some therapeutic help.

The desolation intensified and I started to think it couldn't get any worse; so of course it did. My scorched and blackened soul screamed, gurgled, and shrieked mercilessly. I wailed in prolonged purgatory. *Oh, God, if you are really there, please, please take this pain away. I'll do anything. I'll come back to the Catholic Church.*

Complete bullshit, of course, but my thoughts were racing:

Might have a crack at the Anglicans. Man, do they need a lot of prayers. Hey, no! No! Of course, the United Church of Canada — decent, egalitarian, honest, and a bit loopy. I sometimes wonder if depression is God's punishment for my transgressions and those of others. What other reasons can there be? But I don't believe in God. I'm fucked, I guess.

Well, in the end, Toni's mother didn't die and I was released from AIM after six weeks.

The clubs lay in a heap of weighty memories. The once-sleek irons glistened and thwacked no more. Instead, they lay dusty on the floor of the garage in Muskoka.

There's a nonsensical adage we all know and preach — there are only two certainties in life: taxes and death, in that order. Well, I've got one more: moving house. It will always be a nightmare, one that will weigh mightily on your mind and credit card for months. Toni and I knew this, of course, but we were not prepared for the reality we had chosen to forget — two homely people stared at a basement full of sins of omission, and we were about to pay for it. We had moved across continents, hemispheres, even across the street, a dozen times at least. And we never learned a thing. Well, just that one person's treasure is another person's garbage. It didn't help that most of our basement was full of garbage, not treasures, accrued during a lifetime of travelling around the globe.

But now, after a decade in Muskoka, we were moving, surely for the last time, from the house in the village of Dwight back to a condo in Toronto. Even I could figure out that one five-bedroom house with a basement does not empty into a cramped condo in the big city. Stuff had to go.

I had conveniently forgotten about the garage with its own particular charm of worn winter tires, two broken mowers, one snowshoe, a broken barbecue, a bag of lost-but-not-forgotten kitty litter, piles of damp and yellowed newspapers, mounds of pipes, bars, brooms, bottles, washer fluid, suitcases, cardboard boxes, musty and mouse-eaten books, maps of the world, vermin-chewed curtains, two heaps of clothes for Goodwill, that aforementioned forty-year-old set of golf clubs, a broken desk, two collapsed kitchen chairs only twenty years old … and that was just at first glance.

The rental van seemed big enough, but my friend, mover, and driver Wolfgang looked at the garage, then the basement, and finally back to the van. "We'd better get started," was his succinct, but clearly disturbed observation.

But not even the mighty Wolfgang, a former German tank driver, over six feet tall and I'm guessing three hundred pounds, could have known of the pain to come. Wolfgang and his partner, Eva, had promised to help us with the move. We were trying to save money by doing the whole thing ourselves with a little help from the friendly folks in small-town Canada.

We weren't surprised when all our requests for help met, as usual, with cold rejection. Small-town warmth? Oh, sure, if you've lived there for fifty years or have fifty million bucks to buy your way in to their chameleon culture founded on want and self-preservation. Many in this most Christian of societies defy the myth of good neighbourliness unless it involves money.

"Mow your lawn, mister? Twenty bucks."

"Clear the snow off the driveway? Twenty-five bucks."

There's no garbage collection in Dwight, which has a permanent population of around two hundred, which swells into the thousands in the summer as massive, ostentatious RVs jostle with canoe-wrapped cars headed up Highway 60 to Algonquin Park. City folk are often too lazy to drop their garbage off at the dump and some hurl their detritus outside the corner store, the Dwight Market. Others empty their sewage tanks at the side of the road. Ah, the sweet smell of a Muskoka summer.

The dump itself is a thing of beauty, as far as landfills go. They've just built new bear-proof pits, all spiffy and ultra clean — just the place for the shock of a lifetime. If you've never been, the process is that you stop at an official shed where a grunt tells you to move your vehicle onto the scales properly so it can be weighed full. When you leave, it's weighed again, and presto, credit card jubilee!

It took Wolf and me five sweat-drenched trips to the dump to witness a lifetime of hoarding pouring into one huge bin. The real estate agent had told us to clear away the clutter, and that's all I heard. I went into a frenzy, throwing out everything. Garbage bags were overflowing with my treasures: *There goes a Brother typewriter. Oh, damn! That's a Bluenote jazz LP. Why did I throw that out?*

There were also garbage bags full of books — smelly, damp, musty masterpieces — that had to go. *They did, didn't they? Shouldn't I have kept them? God, I hate this.*

As the sun lowered in the Muskoka evening sky, it was finally done. Wolfgang stared at the receipts given out by the gate collector.

"Jeez. This must be some kind of record!" exclaimed the astounded dump master.

It was. We had just dumped three thousand kilos of nothing — three tons of meaningless memories.

Soon after the move back to Toronto in 2009, I got some more professional work, but unfortunately it again involved a lot of driving. Why was that a problem? Well, during this period I crashed cars — lots of them. That's no surprise to the mental health folks. They know it has to happen. And, boy, were they ever right. A few years ago, I was banned from my rental company because I required five replacement cars in two months. Why is this no surprise? Well, apparently, people suffering from depression are twenty times more likely to have a road accident. Twenty times! I'm told it's due to lack of concentration, a drifting mind, and the dizzying effects of many anti-depressants.

I almost killed myself in one of those crashes, one that destroyed a brand new hatchback. It was a total writeoff — a bit like the driver. I was cruising along the back roads in the middle of snowy winter in eastern Ontario when I hit a patch of black ice. The car was launched into the air, started spinning wildly; then, at seemingly incredible speeds, it ploughed backward up a snow bank, engine screaming, and tipped on its side.

"You'd be dead without your seat belt," said the concerned cop who helped arrange another tow and a ride to the nearest town.

The reason I was driving on these snow- and ice-encrusted back roads in the first place was to get to the First Nations Technical Institute (FNTI) on Mohawk Reserve near Kingston, Ontario. I'd been hired on contract in what would turn out to be one of the most dispiriting and depressing assignments of my life. The downward spiral began before the job even had. In preparation for the course, I had to spend hours with a professor friend re-writing the nonsensical curriculum.

My brief was to bring eight specially selected First Nations students from across the country up to a standard that would allow them to apply to a journalism program at a community college. It was a golden opportunity for the students, all of whom were on generous scholarships from their bands. But something was wrong; I felt it from day one. My first clue that all was not right with this class was when I gave them a news quiz that included some very basic questions meant to test their general knowledge. Questions such as: Who is Joe Clark? What's the capital of British Colombia? Why was Claude Monet famous?

The highest score was a two out of twenty. I simplified the quizzes even further, but still nothing more than a two. And these folk wanted to study journalism at a higher college.

Then they stopped turning up. Some days I would have three, others none. And then I would have to start all over again. I commented to them on this lack of commitment and the demands of journalism until I was wiped out.

Each weeknight I would drink in my hotel room, despondent, bothered, and bewildered. Then every Friday night I would drive the 250 kilometres back to Toronto through frightening snowstorms. Once, I missed a turn-off and went an hour out of my way in the dark. This went on for two months. I was heading in a very bad direction very quickly. *Oh, Christ. Please, oh please, hold me together.*

At FNTI, I was the only non-Native out of about thirty staff and students, and I was ignored by almost all of them. There was no help, no guidance, no interest in what I was doing; not even a hello from the administrators. I could see a disaster roaring down the track. The place felt, looked, and *was* deeply disorganized.

During one of my last trips back from the reserve, in a very old rental car, the brakes failed and I slewed across the road into a snow bank. I have not driven since those dented disaster days, and will never do so again. Mentally ill people should not drive, hard as that may be for them to accept. Tough shit, I say. Look at what I did.

My frustration with the job overwhelmed me when the two students who bothered to turn up to the course one day accused me of racism. Why didn't I teach Native studies? they asked.

"Because my contract says I have to teach you journalism, which will get you further ahead in your own community, but first at one of the community colleges. It's a great opportunity and you guys seem to be wasting it."

But she had a point. I certainly wasn't racist, but no thought was given to their culture when the First Nations members came up with the scholarship idea. No wonder the program was a disaster.

That was the day I quit. I felt naked and beaten and I had experienced overt racism (now I know what it's like).

The final drive back that day was mercifully uneventful until I rattled into a shopping mall. I picked up some groceries, hopped back in the battered old Ford they had reluctantly given me, and turned on the ignition.

Nothing.

I tried again. Not a sound.

"Hello, Enterprise?"

17

THE LONG ROAD TO RECOVERY

So how do I have myself together enough to write this book? The answer to my recent rebound is not the twenty-five years that I spent in mental purgatory, but the break I got recently with two excellent therapists. One is a psychiatrist. He gives me therapy and the desperately needed drugs. The other is a psychologist he recommended. For the record, a psychiatrist can prescribe medications, a psychologist cannot.

The psychologist introduced me to Cognitive Behaviour Therapy, or CBT, which is being hailed as another new miracle cure for depression. Of course, it's not, but it has helped me, along with the drugs, to start leading a fairly normal life, whatever that is.

Without getting too technical, CBT involves the patient analyzing himself directly. In my case, I record my fears and anxieties by writing them down on a prepared chart. I analyze them and write that analysis on the same chart. It doesn't sound like much, but it has worked for me.

Maybe it's just the fact that I'm writing stuff down. Maybe it's the empowerment of the patient.

The clinical point of CBT is to lance the core negative values that comprise depression. This is done in a very slow, methodical manner. The patient starts on the outside of an orbital path, jotting down worries and feelings. This is the start of boring toward the core, where the values are almost always negative. The fears, the doubts, the tears, the shame seem stupid and inane. They're not, of course. They're real symptoms of the depression. But they need a therapist, a skilled counsellor or psychiatrist.

For example, the boss is driving you nuts. She doesn't appreciate you. She thinks your ideas are rubbish. So how do you get rid of this negative thought, and where does it come from? As recently as two years ago I was afraid to go buy a *Globe and Mail* at the corner store because I was scared the woman behind the counter would ask me a question. Worse, I might not know the answer. I was ashamed of my age when a young man offered me a seat on the subway. I was afraid to go to weddings because I did not and could not make small talk with other guests. I fiercely berated myself as a "fucking idiot" when I went out the door of my apartment building that was not as close to the bus stop as another door. You know the old cliché "afraid of his own shadow." That was me.

Here is one of the first thought records I completed. You will see it has negative overtones. They usually do. Otherwise there's no point in doing them.

Thought Record
Situation: At home getting ready to go to first CBT session.
Mood: Nervous, fretful, depressed
Rating of Anxiety: 70 percent
Rating of Depression: 75 percent
Automatic thought: I won't be able to do CBT. It won't work.
Evidence that supports thought: I am older, have memory loss, not sharp.
Evidence against thought: I am still smart. I do crosswords well. I need help.
Alternative balanced thought: I have to try. I owe it to myself. Maybe CBT will help.

Mood after analyzing my situation: I feel better.
Rating of Anxiety: 40 percent
Rating of Depression: 60 percent

So what's the explanation of the above? I write down how I feel in the correct columns:

Situation: I am going to try something new.
Mood: I am scared. I think I am an old useless fart who can't do anything right. Why would this be any different?
Anxiety: Wow. That's bad.
Depression: I feel really down.
Evidence #1: For me there is lots of evidence that shows I can't do CBT.
Evidence #2: There is some evidence that shows my fears are unfounded.
Alternative balanced thought: There must be a thought that's close to the truth.
Mood rating: Write it down, Johnny. Wow, I feel better. Not great, but better.
Anxiety: It feels lighter.
Depression: Not great. But I can handle it.

I was told I had to find a CBT partner. That's a term I had never heard before, but it turned out to be a phrase I would find comforting over the next two years. My psychologist asked me if there was anybody I knew who was a close enough friend, someone who would help me with my CBT training for an hour or two a week. Preferably this person would have some knowledge or training in psychology. He or she would have to be objective. But most of all, he would have to have some time on his hands.

I thought about it for a while and told her I might know someone. His name was David Burt. We had worked together both at Global TV and CBC. He was a reporter at that time and I was the hotshot TV field producer I have previously described. I told my psychologist I vaguely remembered he had studied some psychology at university, but had opted for journalism as a career instead. I hadn't seen him for years, but we had always been close. We did excellent work together, and had always laughed a lot.

"That sounds like your man, John."

"Sure, but will he do it?"

"You can start by asking him."

Well, that sounded easy enough. But I was terrified. When we had worked together, David relied on me to be the best in the world. He knew I was a bit of a nutbar, high strung and all that, but I knew he respected me professionally. A lot of folks did. However, now that I was a useless old nobody that nobody wanted, why the hell would he give up his time for me? I agonized for days, but eventually, with painful, embarrassed "courage," I phoned him.

The bar we agreed to meet at was called the Sunrise Bar and Restaurant, a dark, exquisite palace with flat, upright wooden chairs that stabbed me in the back and tables that rocked like Elvis on a souped-up night in Graceland. The regulars were so regular I reckon the place doesn't open or close without them. They're probably from the sea of apartment blocks flooding the area. Their favourite drinks? Rye and Coke and Budweiser.

I caught a guy in a suit and tie at another table staring at me for a full minute or so every few minutes. *Who is this asshole?* I thought to myself. *I've never seen him in my life. Cheeky fucker.* I was going to go over to him to see what the fuck he was staring at, when I realized that just above my head there was a TV playing sports coverage.

I was suffering heavily from depression that day and terrified of meeting David. *What will I say? Can I sneak out of it? A cellphone call to say I'm suddenly sick? No, he's too smart for that. The bus has broken down! That won't work either. The bar is about five minutes from my condo.*

When he arrived, David smiled broadly and energetically shook my hand. It was a good welcome, nothing phony. Both David and I have spent a lifetime picking up on the flash of a smile or a facial twitch, reading the faces of other folks. I hadn't seen him in years. He was bigger than I remembered; stronger, too.

I felt relatively at ease, but cringed and hated myself when I thought how old and overweight I looked. *Fat, stupid me. God, I hate myself. Even here. Even now.*

That's how I thought.

I was taking a hell of a risk asking David to be my CBT partner. What if he said no? *I don't need this hassle. I should have ...*

(Oops! There's the *should* word. Therapists tell us not to use it. *Should* indicates demands or absolute intransigence, even though it's subconscious. It places an onus on the speaker and the listener. Sorry, therapists.)

My depression was oozing out of my pores and passages so badly. I desperately tried to hide it with small talk for a while, slurring through my drug-dry mouth.

It was around 11:30 a.m., and David ordered a breakfast of eggs and chips. As we were waiting for the food, I knew I had to say something right then, or not all.

Oh, Christ!

I chose that moment, and it turned out to be one of the smartest decisions I've made in a lifetime of fuckups.

I simply said, "I need your help."

For two years now, David has met me every single week and we chat for two hours. He also phones me regularly and is a serious, responsible CBT partner. He understands my illnesses and the theories of CBT; he's learned the medications, the extent of my pain and needs; he senses when I'm up or when I'm down. He's also a close friend, especially now — at least, that's my perspective.

I hit it lucky, big time. Without this combination of healers and therapies, I would still be in hospital. David is always there, no matter when or how, and he has even helped me write this book. He is an incredible support and a continuous reminder of just how far many caregivers will go.

During our sessions, we go over the thought records I have mentioned, but we also talk about some of the things I had been afraid to think about over the years. For example, he had noticed that I had a huge amount of respect for my father. He was right. He asked me what impact he thought that had on me. We talked about how we all have fathers and they all do something for a living. Maybe I was putting the old man on a pedestal? He didn't say that directly. He just asked me questions.

Therapists have to be careful when they treat patients. They can be sued. A CBT partner, however, can be a little more frank and honest, a little more of a friend. But he also must be very, very careful. David often reminds me he's not a trained professional and won't give a direct opinion on a given problem. He says some questions have to be answered by my therapists, not him. However, we do have more personal conversations about my life than I have with therapists, and that might be helping me to range a little closer to my core.

I am not cured yet. And this next story is a lesson on the profound effects of drugs and sleep.

One night recently, after having slept badly for three consecutive nights, I decided to go to bed at 9:00 p.m., early for me, because I knew that I had to meet David at eleven o'clock the next morning.

Well, the alarm failed to go off and I didn't wake up until exactly eleven o'clock. I went crazy. I phoned David to say I was going to be half an hour late. I hurriedly cleaned my teeth and shaved. I phoned him again with an update.

"Make that three quarters of an hour. I'm so sorry I'm late."

David was mystified. He said we didn't have a meeting. I was babbling, not making any sense. Then, shaking with resentment at my own stupidity, I ran for the door.

"What are you doing?" yelled a bleary-eyed Toni.

"I've got to meet David at eleven and I'm half an hour late."

"What are you talking about? That's at eleven o'clock tomorrow. It's eleven o'clock on Thursday night."

I had no idea what she was talking about. The sleep meds were working their hardest at that point and had addled my brain so much I couldn't tell if it was night or day. I looked at the blackness outside. *What the hell? Wow, it's dark for eleven o'clock.* Eventually, after about five minutes, the semblance of truth dripped into my shocked brain.

There's a lesson for caregivers here. If Toni hadn't woken up and explained it all to me, I would have gone out into the dark night on my own. This is a common infuriating occurrence with depression: forgotten appointments, lost books, lost wallets, lost streets, lost houses, lost mind, lost … well, just about everything.

Another night I managed a mere two hours' sleep, so of course the next evening I was exhausted and went to bed at 10:00 p.m. I promptly fell asleep. When I awoke, I bounded out of bed and got dressed. I then slipped and smashed my head against the door. The noise attracted Toni's attention.

"John. What on earth are you doing?"

"Getting dressed."

"John, I don't believe you — you've done it again. It's only eleven o'clock on Thursday night!"

F-u-u-c-k! Yep. As usual, my dump truck brain filled with meds had been weakening me. My sleep was erratic and infuriating. It was after this incident that my psychiatrist decided to replace the irksome drug called Seroquel.

18

THERAPY: WHAT'S RIGHT FOR YOU?

As you may know, most psychiatric hospitals have what they call group sessions. They start with ten or so patients describing to a therapist, and one another, their feelings at that moment. After the round of "feelings," as they call it, there is generally a discussion of techniques patients can employ to increase self-esteem, control anger, and avoid a depression relapse. The problem with all of these lectures is that they are conducted with a group of patients who are foggy, swirling, and leaden with the side effects of various anti-depressants and sleeping medications.

Mindfulness Therapy is one of the latest methods to hit the mental health world, much like Prozac and the SSRIs (selective serotonin reuptake inhibitors) did years ago. Mindfulness Therapy includes a form of meditation that employs discipline and repetition. The books suggest doing it for at least half an hour a day. It not recommended for severely depressed people, and it was only recommended to me after I had improved my mental state with CBT (Cognitive Behaviour Therapy).

Mindfulness Therapy helps a lot of folks. It helps me when I use it. It's difficult when you first start, but basically, you take deep breaths as you inhale and focus your mind on an object, let's say your big toe. Still focused on listening to your breath and thinking only of your toe, you then move up and think about your ankle; after a few minute you then move up to your shin-bone, still breathing deeply and restfully. The aim is to keep this up for thirty minutes, but if you can't make it the full half-hour, screw it; it's whatever you can do. The purpose of Mindfulness meditation is to live in the moment, to shut out the regretful past as well as the frightening future.

Both CBT and Mindfulness Therapy work for me, and they seem to be working for many other patients; although it's hard, hard work, it's worth it.

New Mindfulness treatments are on the horizon. One is called Acceptance and Commitment Therapy, or ACT. It aims to eliminate the way language entangles patients into a futile attempt to wage war against their own inner lives. Through metaphor, paradox, and experimental exercises patients learn how to make healthy contact with thoughts, feelings, and memories that have been feared and avoided.

Let's revisit group therapy. For many it works well, but I have not found it successful personally. One problem is that it brings me down. How can sitting around with a group of other depressed people, some of whom want to commit suicide, help me feel better?

Here's what occurred during one psychiatric aftercare circle that I participated in. There were about fifteen patients in the room, and we were each asked in turn to tell the others how we were doing and what we did to ward off depression. Some patients cribbed their answers from the handout, which made eminent sense, but others just spoke from the heart.

"I feel groggy but a lot better. I would say I'm a six out of ten. I've got a problem with my parents I'd like to discuss with the group if there's time," one patient stated.

Marcie, the therapist leading the group, said they'd try to make time at the end of the session. If not, the patient could see Marcie later in the day.

"Now, Mario. You've been very quiet. Tell us how you're doing and what you do to prevent a relapse."

"Well, it's the same every time I come here. It's a waste of time. Nothing changes. I've got nothing to do. My wife doesn't speak to me. I just sit on the front porch every day from the time I get up until I go to bed."

"And what do you do?" the therapist asked.

"Nothing. I just sit there. Nobody bothers me."

"What about food. Are you eating okay?"

"Not much. I haven't got any money. It goes on rent, so some days I go hungry."

"We can help you. Wait for me after the session and I'll tell you where to get food. Mario, let me change the subject. Do you feel safe? Do you have harmful ideations?"

"What?"

"Do you have thoughts of suicide?"

"All the time. I've got no reason to live. Honestly, I'm not kidding."

"Mario, that is so untrue. I've watched you with the other patients. You interact. You laugh. You chat. Don't you even go for coffee together afterward?"

"Yes."

"Well, Mario, that's a huge step. Why don't you arrange to meet a different member of the group each week and get some company?"

"No. You see, I've nothing to talk about. Nothing. I really don't see the reason for living. I really don't. Oh, Jesus."

"When do you see your doctor next, Mario?"

"I don't have any idea. I didn't make an appointment."

"If you don't mind, Mario, I'm going to make an appointment for you. Wait a minute. Doesn't Dr. Helen do rounds today? Yes, she does. Mario, let's you and I go and find her at the end of group."

"It won't do any good. I've been to her before."

"And you're still here. And we want you with us. You've got so much to offer. So, after group then?"

"Oh, okay. What's to lose?"

He's gotta be kidding, right?

I *want* to tell you that I think group therapy is great, but I would be lying. It works for some, but not for me. Most of the time, nobody has anything to say except for expressing their own misery. It's just so, well, depressing, and my reaction is predictable. And there's no stopping many patients. It's everyone's right to talk and be heard. But I want *my* therapy, not yours. I'm sick. So are you. Too bad. I'm tired of moving to the back of the room so I won't have to listen to the anguish and depressing misery being poured out for one hour each morning.

Once, at CAMH, I was unable to get a word in for four straight sessions. The room was full of bipolars, who tend to take over any situation they're in. Of course, as the saying goes, some of my best friends were bipolar. My therapist and psychiatrist advised me to get the hell out of there because it was negatively affecting my depression, my healing, and my health.

There are obviously benefits to group therapy: camaraderie and self-expression can improve one's demeanour. That's mainly for the not so sick, or the drugged up patients who need it nice and simple. To be fair, the therapists are trying as hard as hell to get their act straightened out. They're brave people.

Holistic medicine is a solution for some people. I have tried some herbal remedies. They don't work for me, but that doesn't mean they won't work for you.

When you talk about therapies, you name it, it's offered. Eventually, I got the gist of doing these Thought Records, and the CBT began to help ease my anxiety, self-esteem issues, and depression. But it has been a long haul.

The best source for information about the different therapies and access to them is, of course, a mental hospital. Toronto is lucky to have the big, research-heavy Centre for Addiction and Mental Health (CAMH). The next best place to seek help is a major hospital emergency. But, oh, god, the ten-hour wait when your brain is bursting!

Finding a good therapist is often a matter of money and luck. Thousands of folks go to therapists, so you might be able to find a good one. In Canada, be prepared to pay at least a hundred bucks (or much more) per session. I would suggest that when you are initially seeking out therapy, you try the free public health system first. Unfortunately, many of their therapists are booked up to a year ahead, so it may be a waste of good energy. But it's worth a try. If you call a private therapist or psychologist, ask what methods they use to treat their patients. You can then search for more information about the techniques they employ by visiting respectable mental illness websites of places like the Mayo Clinic, CAMH, or the Cleveland Clinic.

When I had my "epiphany" with the CBT method, I began to think that there was a chance I might be able to lead a normal life. Not so fast, boy wonder. My psychologist is a great one; she changed my life for the better. She taught me CBT. But I have to do the work. If you keep hunting, like me, you may eventually find that chink of light we all crave.

Some key questions both CAMH and I believe you should ask when speaking with a prospective CBT therapist include: Where did you do your CBT training? How long did you study it? How do you teach it? What materials do you use?

Then ask yourself: Do I feel respected? Is the therapist listening to me?

And the greatest advice I can give you is to trust your gut. If there's any sign of evasion or incompetence, get out — fast. Your mind is at stake. Remember, you are choosing a therapist, not the other way round. Ask questions.

As I have said, until I found my current psychiatrist and psychologist, I was constantly on a search for good therapy. Along the way, I encountered a few doozies. There are a few things that people with depression and their support groups should watch out for when it comes to therapists. For example, one therapist to whom I was recommended had on his table a strangely familiar yellow and black text book: *Overcoming Anxiety for Dummies*. This guy was not a doctor, but seemed to have a degree or experience with counselling. He was a church minister, a lovely, caring man drowning in his own ignorance and pulling me under with him. And he was treating potentially suicidal patients! I left him after just one session.

I also went to a prospective new CBT therapist. I asked him the same questions you read earlier, and within five minutes I knew he was yet another charlatan who had no professional training. I knew more about CBT than he did.

Several years ago, I found the worst imposter of all while searching for a new psychiatrist. What an experience that was. I'll call him Dr. Wanker.

Well, Dr. Wanker was what I call a "shrink," and his main method of therapy was to glare at me for up to fifteen minutes, not saying a word.

This freaked me out to the point that I began to deteriorate dramatically. It's appalling to note that this man is still practicing. If I had my way, I would have him jailed for misrepresentation and causing harm — a direct violation of the Hippocratic Oath. You may notice that Dr. Wanker is only one of two people in the book I damningly call a shrink. I know at least two people going to him, and his methods sound as reckless as ever.

Here's part of the letter I drafted to the doctor after I left him. I never sent it.

> Dear Doctor,
> I wish to protest your behaviour while you treated me for severe, chronic depression. You took advantage of my illness to bully me and intensify the helplessness of depression. In my opinion, you are dangerous and should not be practicing psychiatry.
>
> I thought you would have been fired by now. But I have just been informed that this is not the case.
>
> First, [regarding] your method of mute, staring therapy: I silently screamed and squirmed in mental agony. I wanted to run and hide, swamped with embarrassment, self-loathing, fear and impotence. Each time our sessions ended I left your office shattered and dying inside. But I was too sick to make the logical steps of ending our relationship and reporting you to the appropriate authority.
>
> The day before one meeting, I left a message on your answering machine to say that at 10:00 a.m. [the next day] my company would be announcing major job cuts. Mine was rumoured to be one of the casualties. I said I would have to cut our session short by 15 minutes so I could get back to work to hear whether I had a job or not.
>
> You stormed past me in the waiting room, silent, but your red face and your withering stare emanated decidedly un-Hippocratic hostility. Then you called me in and yelled through your gritted teeth: "Listen! You

just can't come and go as you please! You ring up and say you have to cut our session short because of some meeting. Who do you think you are? It's just not on."

The venom in your attack puzzled me. The meeting was, to me, very important and possibly life-changing. It could trigger another major depression crash. I needed help. I got abuse.

In that session I stated: "You don't care about me, do you? I'm not a person or a patient. I'm just a health insurance number to you, isn't that right?"

"Yes. You are just a number."

I knew the answer, but was still devastated when you uttered it. But it was difficult to comprehend what happened next. I asked you a question. "So this is about money? Would you like me to pay you for the lost 15 minutes?"

I took out my chequebook and started writing. I asked you how much I "owed." You recited the amount and then took the cheque.

I've lost count of the times you kept me waiting and then cut the session short to keep up with you timetable.

To me, you are a profound danger to your patients. You should resign immediately.

I await your reply before deciding if I am going to refer your misbehaviour and malpractice to the College of Physicians and Surgeons.

Yours sincerely,

John Scully

The medical hierarchy is famous for shielding its own. So I felt it was my duty to write this tough but polite letter to the doctor and to the Minister of Health. But, as I said, I never sent it.

I forgive myself. I was still working in the media at the time. I did not want to create any more problems for myself than I was already having. I did not want to become known at my work as the shit-disturbing depressed guy. I didn't need the stigma.

The relationship between patient and doctor during psychotherapy is a unique one, a kind of connection that is unlike any other. In some ways, it can be more intimate than our most intimate relationships, but it also paradoxically values a vestige of professional distance between therapist and client.

Therapists, alas, are just as human as the clients they see, and they come with the same human foibles. They have bad habits, as we all do, but some of those habits have the very real potential of interfering with the process and the unique psychotherapy relationship.

The following is a list of twelve things you should ensure your therapist doesn't do — some of these may actually harm the psychotherapeutic relationship. They were compiled by Dr. John Grohol, of Psych Central.

1. Showing up late for the appointment.

Therapists will usually charge a client for an appointment if they fail to cancel it with less than 24 hours notice. Yet some therapists seem perfectly oblivious to the clock when it comes to [them] showing up on time for appointments. While the occasional lateness may be excused, some therapists consistently show up late for their appointments with clients. Chronic lateness is often symptomatic of poor time-management skills.

2. Eating in front of the client.

Unless you have enough for everyone, eating and drinking during a psychotherapy appointment is considered ill-mannered. Some therapists offer clients the same access to coffee or water that they themselves enjoy. (If you're going to drink something in front of a client, make sure you offer your client the same.) Eating while in session — by client or therapist — is never appropriate (it's therapy, not mealtime). And asking, "Do you mind if I finish my lunch while we get started?" is inappropriate — clients don't always feel comfortable enough with expressing their true feelings.

3. Yawning or sleeping during session.

Yes, believe it or not, there are therapists who fall asleep during sessions. And while an occasional yawn is a normal component of our daily functioning, non-stop yawning is usually only interpreted one way by a client — they are boring the therapist. Therapists need to get a good night's sleep every night, or else they cannot be effective in their job, which requires constant and consistent attention and concentration.

4. Inappropriate disclosures.

Inappropriate disclosures refer to the therapist sharing a bit too much about their own personal life. Most therapists are warned about doing too much disclosure in session with their clients, because it's the *client's therapy*, not the therapist's. Therapists should keep personal disclosures limited (even if the client asks).

5. Being impossible to reach by phone or email.

In our ever more connected world, a therapist who doesn't return phone calls or an email about an upcoming appointment or insurance question stands out like a sore thumb. While no client expects 24/7 connectivity to their therapist (although some might like it), they do expect timely return calls (or emails if the therapist allows that modality of contact). Waiting a week for a return phone call is simply unprofessional and unacceptable in virtually any profession, including psychotherapy.

6. Distracted by a phone, computer or pet.

Therapists will often ask their clients to silence their cellphone before entering session. The policy has to go both ways, or it shows disrespect to the client and their time in session. Therapists should never accept any phone calls while in session (except for *true* emergencies), and they should turn away from any other distractions, such as a computer screen. In a world that increasingly values inattention and multi-tasking, clients seek refuge from such distractions in the psychotherapist's office.

7. Expressing racial, sexual, musical, lifestyle, or religious preferences.

Although an extension of the "too much disclosure" bad habit, this one deserves its own special mention. Clients generally don't want to hear about a therapist's personal preferences when it comes to their sexuality, race, religion, or lifestyle. Unless the psychotherapy is specifically targeting one of these areas, these types of disclosures are usually best left alone. While it might be fine to mention something in passing (as long as it's not offensive), a therapist who spends an entire session discussing favourite musicians or love of a particular religious passage is not likely helping their client.

8. Bringing your pet to the psychotherapy session.

Unless cleared and okayed ahead of time, therapists should not bring their pets to the office. While sometimes therapists see clients in a home office, pets should stay out of the office while they are in session. To the client, a psychotherapy session is a refuge and a place of peace and healing — pets can disturb that peacefulness and calm. Pets are generally not an appropriate part of psychotherapy.

9. Hugging and physical contact.

Physical contact between client and therapist must always be expressly spelled out and okayed by both parties ahead of time. Yes, that includes hugging. Some clients are disturbed by such touching or hugging and want no part of it (even if it's something a therapist might typically do). Both therapists and clients should always check ahead of time with the other before attempting any type of physical contact, and respect the other person's wishes. At *no time* is a sexual relationship or sexual touching appropriate in the psychotherapy relationship.

10. Inappropriate displays of wealth or dress.

Psychotherapists are first and foremost professionals, and any displays of wealth and style should be discarded in exchange for dressing in an appropriate and modest way. A therapist slathered in expensive jewelry is a put-off to most clients, as are blouses or dresses that show too much skin or cleavage. Too casual of dress can also be a problem. Jeans may suggest too casual an approach to a professional service that the client is paying for.

11. Clock-watching.

Nobody likes to feel they are boring to another person. Unfortunately the therapist who hasn't learned how to tell the time without checking the clock every five minutes is going to be noticed by the client. Most experienced therapists have a good sense of how long a session has gone without having to look at a clock until late in the session. But some therapists seem obsessively compulsive about making note of the time, and the client notices (and internally they may tell themselves what they're saying isn't really important to the therapist).

12. Excessive note-taking.

Progress notes are a standard part of psychotherapy. Many therapists do not take notes during a session because it can be distracting to the process of psychotherapy. They instead rely on their memory to cover the highlights of the session after it has ended. Some therapists, however, believe they must capture every detail of every session in their notes, and obsessively note-take during sessions. Such constant note-taking is a distraction for most clients, and some may find that the therapist uses the behaviour to keep an emotional distance from the client. If note-taking is done during session, it should be done sparingly and discreetly.

There's an incredible amount of information on psychiatry for a depressed patient to wade through. The big question is one that is not easy to answer: What will work for me? It may take time to find the one method of treatment that works for you, but I encourage you to keep trying.

I believe the psychiatrist I am seeing now has to be one of the leading mood disorder scientists in the country. I finally made my huge depression about-turn with him. He recommended a CBT therapist, he experimented with my medication, and he treated me like a human being. I realized I was seeing a man who gave me hope. He's not only absolutely professional, but he is also a researcher and an assistant professor at the University of Toronto. He's been a psychiatrist for twenty years. I must admit that in the beginning I thought he had the bedside manner of a brick, and after the first couple of months I had decided to leave. It was my wife, Toni, who insisted I keep going to him. Thank heavens.

"How's your mood?" he asks me every time.

Over the years, our relationship has changed. We're by no means friends, but I believe we trust each other, and nothing's more valuable than that in mental health. If I'm not too sick and my instinct tells me "this is not working," I tell him. I ask a few more questions if I feel I need to, and then leave. No fretting.

I try to give him a summary of events that caused my trouble or triumph since the last visit, for example: "My mood's no good. I can't stop crying,"

"What do you think caused it? Was it all the events or just one?" he will ask.

Then he will analyze the situation and offer very sound advice; not just psychiatry, but also life skills. In fact, I make few life changes now without consulting him, whether they are depression-related or not. For example, once when I was offered a job, I told him about it. He asked me the following questions: Will it be stressful? How anxious will you be? Will you be in a hotel room on your own? How long will you be away?

Once I had answered him, he offered his advice: "Um, you know,

John, it's up to you, but I would strongly advise against it."

In other circumstances, he was very supportive: "That's a great idea. Volunteering! Writing a book! That's sensational."

And, annoyingly, he can take one look at me and know how I'm doing: "So before we end, let's try changing your drugs a bit. We still have to find the right one for you and then add in some therapy."

When I met my new psychologist at AIM more than a year ago, I had a pleasant surprise. For me, depression and the drugs that fight it have made sex a distant memory, and even at my age, I miss it. But it's nice to know I'm still attracted to women. In my imagination, therapists were smart-assed, superior-acting men or drab, contemptuous women. But my new one? She was ... well ... wow, gorgeous!

When I was introduced to her, I had to remember what I was there for — Cognitive Behaviour Therapy. If I was to learn the CBT she was going to teach me, I had to clean up my act and concentrate only on my clinical mind and what was being taught. Sadly, I had to become a "professional pursuer of therapy," and all hints of other worldly desires were driven from my brain.

This took place in a flash as my psychologist, quietly and gently, made it clear what she was about to do — teach me CBT. The reason for her success with me is an extraordinary testament to her training and her personal skills. She was more than empathetic. For months, she concentrated on changing me into a master of this most crucial of disciplines. She had a soft, gentle, yet firm approach. I was never "wrong," but she would improve my answers so they made more sense and challenged my mind. She understood the complexities of CBT more than any book I have come across. I found her a huge comfort, and with an uncanny understanding of the mentally ill, she gave me all the help she possibly could. This is what I need in a psychologist.

She forced me to dig deeper within myself than ever before as I ploughed down inside, trying to find my core negative values, using her hints, cajoling, and help. I never felt like a fool during our sessions. She boosted my self-esteem with the dissecting of the CBT graphs. She knew I was suffering and did all she could to ameliorate the pain through therapy. She would consult other specialists about my case, and even arranged additional treatment. She went, unheeded, miles out of her way to help me.

In short, she was a gem. I got lucky finding a dignified, warm, supremely skilled therapist who has made a major difference in my life. It does happen.

In the summer of 2011, I had a setback, but in the end it all turned out for the better.

I was scheduled to meet my psychologist and psychiatrist at the same time. (Did I mention I have seen fifty different doctors and therapists over the years?) Anyway, I was supposed to meet them at the usual place on Toronto's College Street at 1:00 p.m. I had had trouble sleeping the night before (probably because I was a bit freaked out by the fact we were going to discuss my case), so I had taken two extra clonazepam tablets at about 3:00 a.m. (I had already taken four, which was my normal dosage.)

I slept in a bit the next morning and, because of the extra drugs, woke up a bit groggy. But I carried on and got ready for the meeting; I had breakfast, shaved, and showered. At about noon, I began my trek from the suburbs of Toronto to the downtown offices.

Part of that trek is a bus and subway ride that takes me to a point that's about a half-hour walk to my destination. As usual, I took the bus and subway and decided to walk from there to the office. The problem was that the temperature that day was 37.5 degrees centigrade, which for American readers is in the high 90s. It broke a fifty-year-old record. No shit. You can check it out.

I arrived on time and began my meetings. On the way from one office to another, however, I stumbled. Well, to be more accurate, I fell down. Then I fell down again. Then, when I got to the second office, I fell out of a chair. Both of my high-class caregivers were startled, particularly the psychiatrist, who prescribes my drugs.

So it was off to Emergency at Mount Sinai Hospital. For three days the psychiatrists talked to me and the doctors poked and prodded. They determined that I was okay, but that maybe I should cut back on my drugs, write a log on how much I took each day, and not go for long walks on the hottest day of the half-century.

I now follow that advice.

19

THE FUTURE OF MENTAL HEALTH CARE

The worlds of science and psychology are loaded with complex ideas about the treatment of mental illness — brain operations, talk therapy, medications, meditations, homeopathic remedies. So where does the issue of depression go from here? Around the world, researchers are tackling the problem assiduously, but with one of the lowest budgets in the Western Hemisphere, mental health is left in the freezing aftermath of what was life skidding to death.

There's a new therapy that's being developed to primarily treat PTSD called Eye Movement Desensitization Reprocessing Therapy (EDMR). During the treatment, patients are asked to recall a traumatic event while simultaneously undergoing bilateral stimulation that involves moving the eyes from side to side while following an object (or rhythmical stimulation using either sound or touch). These rapid eye movements are said to dampen the power of the bad memories. Although it remains controversial among some health care professionals, others claim the treatment is fast, safe, and effective. The researchers say that EMDR is most effective when it is used in conjunction with other traditional methods of therapy. I'm neither an ophthalmologist nor a psychiatrist, but it sounds like the new revolution; however, over the years I've seen many of these new wonder drugs and treatments go where they belong — down the drain. This therapy is only in the research stage in Canada and is not yet widely available here.

In Canada, various labs across the country are studying EDMR, depression, PTSD, anxiety, childhood trauma, panic attacks, and other aspects of mental illness.

The Canadian Mental Health Association's (CMHA) Toronto branch reckons it's got a solution to the shortages of money and beds available for the care of mental health patients. It's an inspired, uncompromising stance that hits the nail very hard on the head. The CMHA website states that there are certain main objectives that the mental health community, with the help of government, should focus on. They believe these changes will make the most difference for people suffering from mental health issues, both in Toronto and across North America.

The first objective is to ensure those affected by mental illness have a home. The target is to have 57,000 supportive housing units for people living with the disease. This must include funding for services and supports that will help people choose and keep safe, affordable housing.

Another important objective is to get people back to work. Unemployment among people with serious mental illness is between 80 and 90 percent. Yet individuals with psychiatric disabilities can work if supported employment and supported educational programs are put in place. People who are already working and experiencing mental health problems need access to employee assistance programs.

Many people living with mental illness want to connect with other people with similar experiences and help each other. Mental health systems need to dedicate a percentage of their spending to funding peer support programs for people living with mental illness and for their families. As well, there should be access to more drop-ins, activity centres, community kitchens, and programs that foster a sense of community.

Immigration in Canada is at its highest level in seventy-five years. There is evidence that immigrants' physical and mental health declines proportionately to the amount of time they stay in Canada, due to migration stress, racism, and employment difficulties. These individuals need services that address their specific cultural needs, and newcomer services would help them to make the transition more easily.

There is evidence that people with serious mental illness are likely to die twenty-five years earlier than the general population as a result of poor access to primary health care and different physical illnesses caused by poverty, lack of nutrition, and the side effects of medication. Improved access to primary health care and chronic disease management is necessary moving forward.

Less than 30 percent of people get treatment for mental illness, and 50 percent do not get the services they actually need. According to a recent CIHI (Canadian Institute for Health Information) study on the cost of illness, we spend $8,000–$12,000 each time a person living with bipolar disorder or schizophrenia is admitted to hospital. We have made choices to spend these amounts of money for a ten- to twelve-day hospital stay when the same amount of money would have otherwise provided treatment and support services for a full year or more. It does not need to be this way. In Ontario in 2010, 4,525 people living with schizophrenia or bipolar disorders received support from assertive community treatment teams, which can reduce days in hospital by 64 percent after just one year. Not only do we need to invest more in community mental health services, but we also need to spend smarter and use available evidence to guide our decisions.

Canada spends 5 percent of its health budget on mental health services; far less than most Western countries. Other countries have found political will. New Zealand, for example, increased its mental health share of spending to 10 percent from 2000 to 2010. Moving forward, Canada and other governments need to commit to spending 8 to 10 percent of their health budgets on mental health care.

We also must ensure that there is a well-trained mental health workforce to provide these services. This includes strategies for recruitment and retention of physicians, nurses, and other health professionals as well as peer support workers across the country, and should also include the use of telemedicine to improve access to mental health and primary health care.

Research funding to investigate the causes as well as treatment of mental illness is a pittance compared with other areas of health care. This needs to change, and we need to improve our efforts to ensure that people working in the field are aware of and utilize information about the latest developments and findings.

And finally, we need to address the stigma that is still attached to mental illness. People living with mental illness and their families continue to report stigma and discrimination within the health care system, in workplaces, and within the community. The Mental Health Commission's Anti-Stigma Campaign is a good first step, but efforts will need to be sustained over many years.

In fact, when was the last time you heard of a Run for Depression? You've heard of runs for cancer, the United Way, and heart and stroke. Why not depression?

Stigma is part of the reason it's hard to raise money. Women used to be afraid to declare they had breast cancer. Most of them aren't anymore. But to declare that you have depression is another step. Put simply, if the CEO of a bank has breast cancer, she may say so; if she is suffering from depression, she may not want her clients or coworkers to know.

Scientists know that stigma gets in the way of funding. And research is expensive. One important area of study that could lead to new treatments or even a cure for mental illness is brain research. What if my problem is the way I am wired? What if I could get treatments to change that? But without increased funding for research and training in this field, new discoveries that may help in the future may be delayed and the next generation of neuroscience researchers will not be adequately trained.

A report by the European College of Neuropsychopharmacology (ECNP) claimed private companies were pulling out of the research game due to the challenge of bringing drugs to market. The ECNP called for more investment and changes to the way drug trials take place. Up to 80 percent of funding for brain research in Europe had traditionally come from the private sector; however, pharmaceutical companies were also retreating from the field because of the cost of bringing drugs to market. It takes much longer to develop drugs for mental illness — thirteen years on average — and these drugs have a higher failure rate and are harder to get licensed. Only one new anti-depressant, agomelatine, has been approved in Europe in the past ten years.

As I head toward the conclusion of my brilliant, sparkling, groundbreaking revelations about me, the rest of the world, the mentally ill, and, may I remind you, me, I want to point out some stuff about the human brain.

I take full responsibility for the choices I have made in my life, but am I working with a "full deck" as they say? Is my brain wired like someone not suffering from depression? Maybe not.

The human brain controls the central nervous system and virtually all human activity. It packs a punch that leaves the world's most powerful computers playing mechanical catch-up. Artificial "intelligence" is gaining on us; but will a computer ever cry if another robot fizzles out? No.

The human brain looks like three pounds of spongy grey sausages all wrapped around each other and divided in half. How can this heap of mashed cell-meat work? Why does it go awry? Researchers are faced with an almost impossible task, when you think that the human brain has more than 100 billion nerve cells. Scientists have actually counted them. Each brain cell is connected to around 10,000 other cells. This adds up to a mindboggling 1,000 trillion connections. A trillion dollar bills laid end to end would reach the sun. No wonder scientists are making tough, sometimes heroic efforts to discover the reasons for our impulses, desires, beliefs, and traits.

Developing new psychiatric medications is painfully slow and often the drugs fail. There are a couple of drugs that look as if they are heading toward the market, but although they're being advertised, they're still being tested. There's hope for one called Viibryd, or vilazodone (for depression), and new research into the already available antibiotic minocycline indicates that it may be effective in the treatment of bipolar disorder. But don't rush out to your doctor and demand one of these meds. Not nearly enough is known about them yet.

And the bigger question would appear to be, is depression curable? When I think about those 10,000 trillion cells, somewhere in the furthest constellation of my unconscious, sometimes I believe it's impossible.

But, unlike a robot, I can summon what I might call my indefinable "soul." I can love, hate, create. I can think, come to personal answers, all in my brain. An instrument so powerful, so destructive, yet creative, it is perhaps our greatest mystery. Even so, I have to believe a cure *is* possible.

20

LOOKING BACK, MOVING FORWARD

I'm getting better, at seventy-two years of age. I'm not there yet, but more meds and intensive therapy have strengthened my determination not to try to commit suicide again or end up back in an institution.

I must report that I feel better than I have in about a decade. Happy days are here again. Well, not quite, but I'm on the way, from my suicide attempt at the beginning of this book to a state where the depression is easing. Yet, the worry never stops and I can't predict PTSD triggers accurately enough. But then, my brain is off-centre. I'm probably like other mentally ill patients, but there's a reason. For example, you have to be insane to try to commit suicide. I mean that literally. We should not be wired, none of us, to kill ourselves. We should be wired for survival.

But my wires seem to have been crossed for many years and only now am I beginning to untangle the jammed up electrical impulses that form my destructive thoughts. I am still gripped with an insane drive for unachievable perfection. I'm frozen into the belief that I'm a failure. I try to be assertive, but not aggressive. I try, often unsuccessfully, to stand up for myself despite the absence of self-esteem. If I'm dealing with the disaster called mental health care, I'm pushy. I don't give up. I hate this next cliché, but it's true: "The squeaky wheel gets listened to." Nah, that's not it. But you know what I mean.

Back when I was that wheezy, scrawny kid, I thought I was going to die, and I wasn't far wrong sometimes. I strongly believe it was then, starting at the age of two, that my mental troubles began. Far-fetched? Yes. True? You bet. No one could grow up sick, drugged, and terrified of the world and not be seriously affected by it. The same goes for many kids who've suffered great trauma, such as sexual or physical abuse or a serious physical illness.

My Catholic upbringing didn't help either. It was sheer indoctrination, intolerance, fear, mortal sin, guilt, guilt, and more guilt, the fires of hell, divisiveness, and absolutism. Even so, I didn't eat meat on Friday, just my mom's fish pie, until the Church started to change its mind yet again, defying its own doctrine of the infallibility of the Pope. I didn't believe in Mary's Assumption, and now the Vatican says I'm right. I have a fantasy that Pope Rats will come to my condo to thank me for my insight and guidance in Catholic doctrine. But he will fail to even say "Ta" for my stand against his homophobia, duplicity, and naiveté. My complete loss of "faith" in the Catholics occurred when they rescinded the major liberal reforms of the early 1960s. The Church has been attacking "liberals" ever since. That merely added to my gathering belief that there is no God as perceived in the fairytale copycat Holy Books of the world's religions.

I want to believe, desperately. It's a reason to die. But I don't. Perhaps there is a "super thing" out there. No one has any real idea. No god? Hmm. Should I hedge my bets?

Pope Rats may have failed, but that's holy water under the bridge compared with a far more painful realization: I had failed my New Zealand family big time. I felt I didn't live up to my parents' expectations. But where did those expectations come from? Yes, from my dad, of course, but also from sports-crazy New Zealand.

The sports bit's easier to explain: I fantasized the same movie as every Kiwi kid growing up — to play for the country's international rugby team, the fearsome, mighty, revered, hagiographic All Blacks. Dad, too, was rugby mad, screaming first at the radio and then at the colour television set, cranked up to the volume of an Apollo rocket: "Oh, Jesus, Christ. Don't kick, you stupid bastard! Run. Oh, Jesus, look at that!"

As my own secret All Black, I was a hero, single-handedly blowing away the French defence and the South African attack while scoring four tries in the process. In reality, I was a thin, underdeveloped kid the howling Wellington wind could blow over in one gust. I never got past the second class of any team group. But once I missed the selection games for that Wellington Midget A team because of asthma; Dad made one phone call and I was in, black jersey and all — The Mighty Midget.

I could run around home and be laid flat with an asthma attack, or it could even happen when I was sitting a movie theatre, but strangely I never had to leave the rugby field because of asthma problems, even in the fiercest weather. Could some sports be a form of mindfulness? A complete distraction? Probably.

My dad came to every game I played and then would come home and replay to the whole family the great game I played, minute by minute, right or wrong. He was a compassionate bulldozer. He gave free legal advice to the disadvantaged, but his sentencing habits were severe. They called him Ben the Hanging Judge, even though New Zealand didn't have the death penalty. He was judiciously exact, and for a boy educated in the perverted schools of Southland, who then put himself through law school and reached the heights of the legal profession, well, he had to be an over-achiever. *Hmm.* Like father, like wee Johnnie.

Only one of my sisters stayed in New Zealand; two went to live abroad, as did I. The country drove us out with its Neanderthal social and insular attitudes, for sure. But so did our upbringing.

I look back on my teen years now with a still-bitter perspective. A university education was not vital, but I wanted to be a doctor. Mom, Dad, and the odious family priest decided I was too dumb to study any further, so into the newspaper business I went: very encouraging. But then the adrenalin kicked in and I was fired up, tearing around the newsroom and the city. I was hooked on the action and began to be obsessed with the work in my quest for professional perfection. As I wrote, that quest took me to the seat of snobbery, England. The chase was on and I was winning. Or so I thought. And I was proving all those defamatory Kiwis wrong. That was one of the driving impulses in my obsession. As I achieved a high degree of success, my parents explained it by telling people, "John? Oh, he was a late developer."

I have no doubt my dad suffered from severe depression and maybe also the unheard of (at the time) PTSD. Both conditions were swamped and covered with booze and hostility. He was a mass of wild contradictions, abusing us and ranting away at the dinner table, but at five the next morning, driving me to the local links to teach me to play golf. Way, way back in the recesses of both our minds, I think, lurked another dream for me, as a pro golfer. But I was never better than above average. His never-stated kindness and his worry about my health and progress, or lack of it, were, in retrospect, touching, but he could not bring himself to say any of this aloud. His boorish behaviour, his fanaticism, his depression, and his admirable achievements seem to mirror much of my life. It's not that I'm blaming him, not really. There is certainly some resentment there, but I'm finally learning where and how my mess of a life evolved into disaster.

The day my dad died I was in Ho Chi Minh City. I flew to New Zealand and landed on a dismal, wet winter's day. During the flight, I felt indifferent to his death. I had still not come to terms with my childhood or his inexplicable behaviour. And I felt guilty about my lack of emotions.

On the way in from the airport in Wellington, one of my sisters asked, "Do you want to see him, John? He's laid out at the funeral chapel."

"No," I replied with an abruptness that surprised me. It conveyed lack of interest, non-concern, and even dismissiveness. My own dad! I could handle looking at my mom when she died, but not him.

I feel much better about Dad now that the years have dimmed the anger and I think I've lit a flame of memory that burns and curls, intertwined in brilliance and brutality. I understand my father's undoubted depression better, I feel more compassionate, and I have a lot more respect for him — the right kind of respect.

I always loved my mom, and I miss her to this day. But after her funeral, it was one of my sisters who remembered, with surprising bitterness, that neither my mother nor father ever expressed their emotions. "You know what? They never hugged us once in our lives. They never held us. They never, ever kissed us."

Standing back, I ponder my own inadequacies, memory loss, aging, boredom, death fixations, timidity, and fear — fear of again getting on the wrong bus and getting off at the wrong stop or of dropping a bottle of shampoo in the drug store. Add to that my trouble focusing, poor concentration, and lack of sleep. Most of us experience mundane or serious problems like these. Sane folks size up the situation and act appropriately. They're absolutely normal events that happen to every-body, but erudite old me turns each of them into a catastrophe. I know my brain balance is askew and I have made judgments that were poor and ill thought out. I'll blame depression, not my inability to settle down, slow down, think, and achieve a balanced perspective. That goes not just for my work life, but my entire life.

If I didn't have illness and depression, I reckon I would have gone to university or, even if I had stayed a journalist, I would have had a much calmer, balanced, and sanguine view of the world. If I were not depressed, for example, I would never have gone back to New Zealand, and I would have stood up to the bullies at other jobs. I would be a much better per-son and father. See, I'm blaming depression again. Reckon it's valid?

For family caregivers of those suffering with mental illness, the strain is often unbearable, and it's not uncommon for them to become depressed, too, and frustrated. Many are at their wit's end as they try to convince a loved one he needs treatment or stop him from committing suicide. You are dealing with life and death, long-term or short. If you're lucky, your city will have ample psych beds. If not, there's that heinous practice of throwing us in prison.

"It's okay, he's nuts."

Sometimes depressed people have infuriating habits. I think only about myself most times to the exclusion of all else. I have been through periods when I don't talk to anyone, or can't. I have cancelled social engage-ments at the last or first minute. I have acted irrationally and applied for a job as CEO of Chrysler. I have sat hunched on the couch in front of the television for hours with no sound on. And here's a deceptively big one — when I'm out walking when I'm depressed, I stare at the pavement and avoid the world. If I lift my head up, my perspective will change. I practise it every day, and it works. But what works best for me isn't just keeping my head up, it's an array of drugs and therapy and now people.

Most of my life I was a fish out of water, but good people got me off the hook. As I have said, one of them was my psychiatrist, who uttered miraculous, even magical words just days before I finished this book: "John! I've never seen you look so good. Your speech is fine and your mood is up."

Dare I tempt fate and declare I'm heading in the right direction? Suicide is now a distant memory. But before I get complacent, I need to consult a few boozy mates: *Dear toothless Allah, antsy Abraham, depressed Jesus. Boys, as you know, I don't believe in any of you, but please, please, please, keep the suicide away. I'll do the rest.*

Of course, I hate retirement — or semi-retirement, or whatever label you want to affix to my forehead. It still grieves me. Like all severely depressed patients, I get bored too easily. What the hell do I do now that I'm trudging down the final path? The big money that beckoned from across the Atlantic has long gone, along with my ability to get some form of work or "play." There are still sad, sad days when I stare at the wall for an hour or so. I'm on the highway to death. So is my family. Today? Tomorrow? God, I loathe those thoughts. They scare me almost frenetically.

So now what?

"Get out and do something new," advise the doctors.

One suggested a train excursion to the 'burbs; anything to get me moving. But a commuter train? Really?

So how do I fill my days? Although it's still dominated by drugs and doctors, I do try to go for an hour-long fast walk most days, down one suburban street and up the other, and then back — very uplifting. In the warm summer sun, the walk can be definitely mood-changing. Other days I go for a swim at a community pool. That takes up about an hour. Cheap movies with Toni are kept for a Tuesday afternoon, no matter how bad they are. The meds can still put me to sleep through the whole film, anyhow.

Although my medication count is down from the high twenties to about eighteen, I sleep better, am not so hungover, and have lost that twenty pounds caused by the bloating effects of the Seroquel, which has been deleted from my song sheet. I'm better for it.

I tried to volunteer with five different organizations recently, including CAMH's clothing shop. I was rejected by every one of them — food kitchens, street outreach, letter writing — I have no idea why. I haven't had as much as a parking ticket in forty years. But volunteering is obviously out.

I even went to the local library recently to learn how to write poetry from a series they were staging once a week. I thought it might help me dig deeper into my brain and come up with more original thinking and, therefore, better prose. It was a chaotic, rambling mess during which not one poem was studied or hints given. There were folks who genuinely benefited and enjoyed the sessions. It just wasn't what I'd expected at all. I didn't go back.

I went to play Bingo once (I still cannot believe it). The space at the community centre was like a large, rather grim empty schoolroom, illuminated with fluorescent lights. The game started an hour late, but that didn't matter to the twenty-three women and two men, including me. Looking back, it was neither fun nor interesting, except for the people. All those women, aging faster than me; some were balding, a few used walkers, but all were intent on their Bingo cards. I guess many of them are lonely widows, and even two hours of Bingo is better than staying at home, ruminating and hurting so privately. There was despondency in the hushed air that never crackled with excited calls or friendly arguments. A dedicated few had brought their own markers and reserved their lucky seats. They clearly loved it. But when the last number had been called and the cheap prizes awarded, everyone got up, scuffing and scraping the chairs, but otherwise drifting out in complete silence.

"We told you to do something completely different," said the doctors. "I don't think we meant Bingo," they amended.

They were right. It was a depression trigger.

I am still advised not to watch the news, especially the world disasters and wars that remind me of my own past, or films about the world ending. I'm supposed to watch only comedy on film or television and I'm not supposed to read the front page of any newspaper. It can trigger depression and PTSD.

No front page? No wars? Only comedy? What a price. But I must admit I peek an awful lot. Naughty Johnnie, but I can't give it all up. Depression is also an addiction of sorts. It grips and craves your most sorrowful thoughts. Quitting "cold turkey" is ... well, don't do it.

My love of music has not returned, although I am working on it. There are hints of enjoyment now with the few other loves of my life, like books. I'm an aimless pain in the ass, without purpose or direction except my obsession with my illnesses. What would I do without them?

But good news: My dreadful memory loss has finally been attributed not merely to aging but mainly medications and depression! I had an MRI brain scan. Empty. Actually, it's better news than that: the brain they did see bore no signs of anything bad like dementia or Alzheimer's. Still, I'm getting a memory test done. Hey, that's something else to do.

I've finally worked up the courage to have lunch and coffee with a few former friends. It was great fun, despite my fears and trepidation. I have to keep meeting people, one of the hardest things I know.

I'm not complacent, and the past year has actually seen me improving all the time. The psychologist wanted me to rate my mood out of ten. I've monitored for the last year, every day. It consistently reads a bit like this: Morning 2.5 rising to 4.5 during the day. I hit 6 once. That is astounding for me. These are my own assessments, but they're not going to be far wrong. Often I go for days at 5.5.

I do rant about mental health's appalling lack of money, beds, respect, and dignity, and the whole stigma thing. AIM was the revolutionary way to approach mental illness, and wildly successful. So why are they cutting back? They used to have twenty-four beds, but then had to close half of them so emergency street cases could have a bed; destruction of a dream fomented by myopic, ignorant politicians, disgraceful budgets, and indifference.

Another thing I'm thinking of doing is learning Arabic. That, or do-it-yourself frontal lobe surgery. Wait a minute. Arabic is out. My psychiatrist and I considered the hours it would take, including travel.

"I'd have to leave home at 5:30 p.m. and get back around 11:30 p.m." I told him.

"So you'll come home hungry, exhausted, buzzing, and obsessed. You won't get to bed for a couple of hours and you will have just wrecked your sleep pattern."

Arabic is out then. So is my psychologist. I can't see her any more — shortages and so on. Now I have to go shopping for a new therapist in the nearest fake psychologists' market. Might as well; the waiting list for real ones is about a year.

To be honest, I still feel angry every day. Not just because of the mental health system, but because there are other wildly wayward spinning thoughts boring into the depths of my brain and refusing to budge. Compulsions like not being late for an appointment; my CBT future or lack of one; the dog that bit me in Israel (apart from a broken leg in Beirut, this was my only injury in the field); and, always, the depression, anxiety, and PTSD. They will not stop. My brain buzzes incessantly with thoughts of worry and doom. I still break down, but not nearly as much as I used to.

Despite these impediments, I think I'm way better. And for that I am grateful to so many individuals. I still have my CBT partner, David, to rely on, with at least one vital meeting each week and phone calls when I feel I need psychological help.

So, ultimately, what's the big secret to escaping all of this? The secret to getting better? How did I improve my depression and other psychiatric illnesses so I could function again? How did I get well enough to write a book, when just a year ago I whined to the nurses at CAMH that I'd never be able to write one word again? And, now, there may be emerging a tinge of joy, less sadness, and perhaps some real hope.

The secret?

I had to work at it.

It's been an extraordinary journey. The best and the worst all rolled into one colonial boy. Today I've progressed a long way past the suicide attempt and my only big worry right now is flashbacks. But I believe I'm out of danger. And a psychologist gave me a great, simple anti-suicide trick. He told me to pin a picture of my family to my shaving mirror so that every morning I'll see what I have to live for.

I now live for my family, not my job, although, honestly, I would still love to cover the world's biggest stories. But I know I can't. I now see how much the family I tended to ignore in the past means to me. There was frequent friction when I came home all washed up, bad-tempered and impatient for the next documentary, but there were also times of great warmth.

John and his wife Toni — together forty-eight years and counting.

It was Toni who carried the load. She brought up the kids, had them educated, bought and sold houses in my absence, and really was a single mom. My family sustains me now, gives me the oxygen and courage I need to survive. Toni has been at it for forty-eight years. Talk about a caregiver who knows her work. It is a never-ending, exhausting, and heartbreaking job making sure I don't fall off the edge. She coddles, cajoles, and, dare I say, cuddles me. Plus, she gives me the occasional kick in the bum, which, ruefully, is generally well-deserved but poorly received.

Jerome, my son, is an inspiration. He's an outstanding Spanish speaker and scholar, and although I think I might have passed a lineage of depression down to him, it doesn't stop him from creaming me at Scrabble or sighing tolerantly when I asked for the eight-millionth time how to fix my computer.

Jerome has more remnants of our Catholic upbringing than the rest us, but he despises Pope Rats and the right wing of the Vatican, as do I, with its history of bigotry, homophobia, and sexual cover-up. But Jerome is also allied with many faiths and NGOs through his translation work and activism.

Here's the ultimate expression of how I feel about Jerome. Once, I was in very bad shape while I was giving a training course for eight hotshot reporters. I was nervous and scared. How to calm myself? I thought of Jerome, and then wrote at the top of every teaching page the initials C.D.G. — Calm. Dignity. Grace. I love him and Emma both dearly.

It's true what the cliché says about "daddy's girl." Emma has sparkled and shone throughout my life. Both the kids make me laugh or can gently bring me down from my self-vaunted place. Recently, I had zoned out while waiting for a bus. Unthinkingly, I turned around and there was Emma. We gave each other two huge hugs, and from then on I was a very happy old pushover. Like her brother, she's got a great mind. She's quick. She's funny. She says my absences made them more independent growing up.

Her wedding speech was the most touching and gentle I've yet to hear. But then I may be a tiny bit biased. As I mentioned earlier, she has a son, Liam, my grandson. I never thought I would be a grandfather. Sure, Liam's the cutest little imp on the earth. Sure, he gives me goosebumps of wonder and delight. So it's no surprise that I don't like him one bit. And, of course, I would never dote on him or give him forbidden fruits like chocolate. And he doesn't like me either.

He calls me John: "Mommy, why is John so silly?"

And, as I mentioned earlier, there are the two cats. Both are so stupid they fixate me.

Those are my loves, and they climb over the depression much of the time.

John's children, Jerome and Emma.

I realize that depression and dealing with it has become my life. It's not that it's my friend; in fact, it's my life-long enemy. But maybe I wouldn't know what to do without it. I imagine some shrinks think I use it as a security blanket. They are partly right. But if they think any mental patient can just throw away his blanket at will, they should go back to school — maybe law school.

Even some therapists who deal with mentally ill people all their careers don't really understand what's going on in the heads of their patients. Mentally ill people don't always make good judgment calls. But, as we've seen, neither do many psychiatrists and psychologists.

But back to my point: What would I do without depression? Well, my first answer is I would try to get work. To be honest, I still want to get back in the field every time I see a good story developing. Oh, to have been in Egypt or Libya as the old despots were thrown out of office!

But as far as I know there are not too many seventy-year-olds working for CNN in the field. And I guess the experience would throw me around the twist.

I could teach, but I am tarnished with the stigma of mental illness, and this book will certainly make that clear to anybody who had any doubts. Who would take a chance? Speaking engagements would be good, and I think I could handle them. Maybe that is more realistic.

I guess what I'm really looking for is a life where I'm content. It's important to stress that as I write this I feel better than I have in about ten years. I'm still troubled, but I am working on it. And yes, I know no one is really content all the time.

Throughout this book I've been brutally honest — painfully so. I've admitted catastrophes even my therapists didn't know about. I've done this so you will see as a patient, or a friend or relative of a patient, that you are not alone. There are ways to ease the pain, even lift the depression altogether.

I hope my journey helps people touched by depression and I hope it helps those who are trying to admit they have the disease and need help. And I guess I will just have to continue living with the big question: Am I sane yet?

EPILOGUE

If I'd known how difficult it was going to make the first three months of 2012, I never would have opted for electroconvulsive therapy, also known as ECT or shock therapy. The idea had always scared the hell out of me. Over the years, I had spoken to too many patients who had suffered memory loss way beyond the level that was outlined as possible by the doctors. My memory was miserable enough, so I always said that I didn't need any shock waves to make it worse.

So why did I change my mind and decide to take the plunge into ECT? Honestly, it was out of desperation. I was not convinced the medications I was taking were having any effect on my depression, anxiety, or PTSD. I had even tried a couple of the newer anti-depressants — Abilify and Cymbalta — but they were of no help.

As it turned out, it wasn't the medically induced fifty-second seizure that was the problem — the mental health profession learned a long time ago that the secret to humane treatment with electric shocks was a general anaesthetic that relaxes the patient's muscles and prevents physical damage when the shocks are administered. That part was actually quite nonintrusive and less painful than going to the dentist. What I didn't bargain for was the one-month titration period — the time it would take to wean me off all my various medications. My small five foot eight inch body rebelled by throwing me into full drug withdrawal — cramps, nausea, diarrhea, insomnia — as it flushed out the benzodiazepines, anti-depressants, anti-psychotics, and the sleepers, all the junk I had been shovelling down my throat for a full decade.

Where're the meds? I want the fix! cried out my aging temple.

Another unwanted side effect of this titration was a sharp spike in my blood pressure. I have a history of hypertension but, as an off-label bonus, it was being controlled by the Nardil, my anti-depressant. I am well aware of the risks that can accompany high blood pressure — heart attack, stroke, and so on — and I felt the doctors could have been more aggressive, but with three new medications we eventually got it down to an acceptable, consistent level.

One unplanned benefit of the titration was weight loss. Many drugs, especially some anti-depressants and steroids, can cause the pounds to pile on. Well, sort of. Although the drugs may slow the metabolism and cause water retention, the fact is that an improvement in mental health often means an improvement in appetite. Some of the drugs can cause weight gain in one patient and weight loss in another. In the latter case, they trick an already confused brain into thinking that the body is still hungry, despite the fact that nausea may make the sight of food intolerable. In the first three weeks of titration, I lost about thirty pounds, and although this is not a recommended diet regimen, I was relieved. I had put on that extra load years earlier, and no matter what I did, I could not seem to shed it. Not even one, two or even three hours of fast walking followed by swimming in the local community centre had made any difference. I had developed a beer belly, not from beer, sadly, but from the Seroquel, which, together with the Nardil, had helped my waist size balloon from thirty-two inches to more than thirty-six.

But, unknowingly, my walking regimen was getting me in shape for the ECT ordeal. I'm sure that's how I managed to sustain the rigours of the full therapeutic course.

Although at one point during the titration I was having serious doubts about my mental and physical stamina, I had passed a point of no return — I'd already come too far and endured too much to reverse my decision. ECT was the only major therapy I had not tried. I realized that for years, I, too, had been caught up in the stigma attached to ECT.

Days before my first trip to ECT, the CAMH team of doctor, anaesthesiologist, and nurse briefed me thoroughly and answered all my questions. They were upbeat and friendly, yet professional. The team insisted that ECT works in about 70 to 80 percent of cases and repeated a fact that I'd heard a great deal — that it is the most effective form of treatment for various mental illnesses, especially depression, bipolar disorder, psychosis, and other mind/brain problems. And, basically, it's the last resort for the treatment of depression and its allied illnesses if the drugs fail. That wasn't very reassuring.

At CAMH, I, like every prospective ECT patient, was shown that pleasant video of the procedure that I mentioned earlier in the book. Though its purpose is to demystify and de-stigmatize shock therapy, CAMH still has its share of critics who claim that the treatment is barbaric and point out that the long-term effects are unknown.

I spoke to a number of patients who'd had a course of nineteen ECT treatments or more, but there was little consistency of experience among them. Some had noticeable memory loss, but for others it was minimal.

I was told I had to fast the night before each treatment, with no food or liquid after midnight. This is because the anaesthetic relaxes all the body's muscles, including the bladder and the bowel. *Ahem.*

On the morning of my first treatment, at 7:15, a lab technician took my blood; then a nurse escorted me from the MAUI unit, down five floors and into the ECT waiting room. Other patients were also arriving for the procedure. The group included both men and women, and they ranged in age from early twenties to mid-seventies. The overwhelmingly majority, however, seemed to be older women. I should note that they also appeared to be from all socio-economic strata: depression doesn't check your bank balance before striking.

The nurse poked her head around the door and called me into the "operating room" where the therapy would be performed. The room looked like any ordinary O.R., relatively drab. The nurse rubbed gel on half a dozen points of my unshaven skull. They attached more electrodes over my heart. These would deliver the jolts of electricity in what is known as a "unilateral" — a less powerful current that is meant to minimize loss of cognition and memory. Many patients go on to have bilateral jolts, but at that point, not me.

"Okay, John, you'll feel a bit of a scratch. That's the intravenous drip for the anaesthetic," the nurse told me.

That's a scratch? Ouch!

The team ran through their checks.

"Dosage?"

"Check."

"Blood pressure?"

"Check."

"Oxygen absorption?"

"Check."

"Heart?"

"Check."

"Pulse?"

"Check."

"Nice deep breaths now," requested the nurse, Jo-Anne, as she placed the oxygen mask over my face.

"Okay, John, you'll be going off to sleep now. Deep breaths."

The last words I heard were added for comfort value by Jo-Anne: "Off to sleep now. We'll take good care of you."

Then nothing.

"Would you like a juice, John?"

Huh? It's over?

I was in the recovery room. I had no idea how long the procedure had taken. Twenty minutes, I later reckoned. *What's that? Oh, God. I've wet myself. Damned muscle relaxant!* And I had only had the tiniest sips of water to combat a drug-dry mouth. The accident repeated itself, and although I was paranoid about drinking any liquids, that morning proved that I had no recourse but to sip even less water in future, if that were possible — and bring a change of clothes with me.

"Do you know today's date?"

"The twenty-third," I answered.

"And what month?"

"February."

"What year?"

"2012."

At least my memory seemed okay.

My day nurse at MAUI came down with a wheelchair. They were meticulous about making sure that I was accompanied by a professional for at least two hours after the anaesthetic. I felt a bit spacey and quite sore. The muscles in my back, neck, temple, eyes, and thighs hurt from clenching during the seizure, and there was nausea, not helped by Tylenol 1s.

When I wrote this section, I had logged ten ECTs and was due an indefinite number more. It's disconcerting that scientists don't actually know why or how it works apart from the fact that the brain is given an almighty wake-up call. Whether it listens or not depends on the individual. And my memory still seemed to be intact.

Scottish researchers have claimed that ECT works by "turning down" an overactive chemical connection between areas of the brain. They say that if we understand more about how ECT works, we will be in a better position to replace it with something less invasive and more acceptable. But they remind us that ECT has been around since the 1930s, so progress is indeed slow.

I continued with the treatments as an out-patient, and I received what was called a weekly maintenance dose. This had its own tribulations, such as having to get up at 5:00 a.m. to make it to the Queen Street West site before 7:30. Again, CAMH was insistent that a friend or relative pick me up after each therapy because of the increased risk of falls if there was any dizziness. Also, there was the potential disturbance to concentration, rational thought processes, hence the possibility that I would not even be able to recognize the right bus or streetcar to get on.

But just five hours after therapy one of those days, I sat at my computer, recalled pretty much how the morning unfolded, and wrote about it. What had surprised me on that visit was the sheer number of patients receiving ECT. The overflow spilled out into an adjacent seating area. That, I understood, went on all week.

Before each treatment, I was given a new test called — and here comes one of those dreaded acronyms again — QIDS, or Quick Inventory of Depressive Symptomatology. It measures a range of depressive symptoms, memory, mood, sleep, appetite, frequency of thoughts of death or suicide, interest or lack of it in once-enjoyed pastimes, and so on. My results were measured against the previous week's, and progress or lack of it was logged. After the ECT and about an hour and a half in recovery, I was given a mainly oral test. The maximum score on the QIDS scale is 27, and the higher the score, the worse one's depression. My score that day was 19, which was not stellar, and although I tend to be conservative in evaluating my own mood, it gave me more reasons to doubt the efficacy of the therapy.

I was a bit startled at the time that I didn't feel as though I'd progressed. Yet my health care providers, friends, and family all told me that my old sharpness had returned, that I exuded a lot more energy, and that I generally looked like a healed human being. But that wasn't how I felt. The side effects of the ECT were still troubling. As well, I was no longer taking any anti-depressants. The perceived improvement could have been a result of coming off the medication, especially the benzodiazepines and Nardil. Or, in my opinion, it could have been a combination of varying factors, including talk therapy, proper sleep, and the absence of drugs, some of which had plunged me into near comas in the past.

I must admit, I hadn't had the stunning reversals experienced by other ECTers I had spoken to. I still have a lasting image of a fellow patient beaming with happiness.

"ECT is incredible. I wish I'd had it years ago," she had gushed.

A month later, my QIDS scores were still way too high, so I made another daring decision — I opted to have bilateral ECT. The doctors warned me that my memory would suffer, but if I was to benefit from the therapy, I didn't think I had a choice. My mood was not in tatters, but neither was it where I wanted it to be. I was still very irritable, morose, and worried. I was determined to give it the best shot I could, even if that meant getting both sides of my brain zapped.

I was concerned about the side effects, of course: headache, severe confusion, muscle ache, and feeling "spacey." These are bad enough with unilateral ECT, so I wouldn't have been stunned if I felt quite lousy afterward. There was some talk of me going back on the meds, maybe the Nardil, or possibly one of the tricyclic anti-depressants such as nortriptyline with a lithium booster, but having just come off all my psychiatric helpers, I was in no hurry to go back to a drug regimen. Without the meds, my weight had stayed off, although my appetite was running amok — sometimes I was ravenous, other times I had no interest in food at all. Booze was a huge no-no, according to the doctors. *Rats!*

I should mention that while all this was going on, I also had surgery in each eye to remove cataracts and to implant corrective lenses. The result was that I now had 20/20 distance vision, but needed cheap glasses for reading. Fellow-ECTers opined that I looked like a professor or an academic. I did nothing to disavow them.

The ECT therapy was covered by OHIP, the government insurance plan, but I discovered that each ECT treatment costs the plan around $500, so at that point I was already well into the thousands of dollars toward hopefully improving my disposition.

After my first bilateral treatment, I sat down to write:

> *Well, I've just had my first bilateral treatment. Those warnings about memory loss were well-founded. When I woke from the anaesthetic, I couldn't remember where I was. I did recognize the nursing staff, but I felt quite disoriented. However, one of the nurses who got me an ice-cold orange juice from the fridge to quench my raging thirst helpfully told me that it went well. She said I had had "a good seizure."*
>
> *Before putting me under this time, the doctor again raised the possibility of me going back on medication, especially since lately I'd been suffering from severe insomnia, and that morning had amassed my highest QIDS score ever.*

I was not a perky pixie. But I wanted to see how my brain would react to the heavier jolt of electricity. Also, I was about to make a new attempt at achieving mental peace with another crack at CBT (Cognitive Behaviour Therapy) with a new therapist, one recommended by my psychiatrist.

My mood is not good at this moment and I am even having trouble writing this relatively simple paragraph.

I had another ECT session two days later, just before that CBT consult. When I re-read the above entry, I thought it clumsy. Self-criticism is one of the bedrocks of depression, but knowing that is of little help.

My wife, Toni, came back from lunch with a very old friend who asked about my health, physical and mental. Toni brought her up to date.

"He's having ECT," she told her.

"What's that?" her friend asked.

"Electroshock therapy."

"My God! Shock therapy! But that's terrible! Isn't it very dangerous?"

"No, no. It's not like the old days. It's the most effective treatment there is for severe depression."

Our friend, and others, still believe in the *Cuckoo's Nest* depiction and assume ECT is barbaric and, literally, maddening. And yet she is a highly educated, bright, aware, and cosmopolitan woman. Other similarly urbane friends have also reacted with the same mistaken horror and disbelief. I guess I've still got a lot of work to do.

One damn movie!

It's now several months later. Once the regimen of ECT therapy was done, I was still not experiencing the results I had hoped for and decided to try a different therapy, one which scientists don't fully understand (how very comforting). It's called repetitive Transcranial Magnetic Stimulation, or rTMS. Over a period of a month, I lay in a reclined chair twenty separate times while a nurse-technician hit me with her best magnets. That is, she held a black magnetic coil about the size of a standard pound of butter, placed it against my head, and turned it on. I was not under anaesthetic this time, and it felt like having short bursts of a mini pneumatic drill pounding the upper right side of my head. Trust me, it was not very pleasant at all. Each of five bursts lasted about forty seconds with a break of about a minute in between. Within fifteen minutes, the session was over. It's thought that the pulses stimulate nerve cells in a specific part of the brain believed to control depression. It took eighteen of the twenty sessions and roughly 3,500 electric pulses before I felt a slight improvement.

Ah, but there's more. Magnetic Seizure Therapy (MST), which CAMH told me about after I had undergone the rTMS, is the new, better-behaved cousin of ECT. Unlike traditional shock therapy, it doesn't cause a full brain seizure, just a localized one. But it still requires the patient be fully anaesthetized. I haven't decided when or if I will opt for this one yet.

My reticence over MST proves one thing, I suppose. Am I sane yet? You betcha.

(Well, maybe.)

RESOURCES

BEFRIENDERS INTERNATIONAL
Worldwide organization dedicated to suicide prevention, with links to various resources and helplines all over the world.
www.befrienders.org

CANADIAN ASSOCIATION FOR SUICIDE PREVENTION
www.suicideprevention.ca

CANADIAN MENTAL HEALTH ASSOCIATION (CMHA)
www.cmha.ca

CENTERS FOR DISEASE CONTROL AND PREVENTION (CDC)
(Heads Up Initiative)
www.cdc.gov/concussion/HeadsUp/youth.html

CENTRE FOR ADDICTION AND MENTAL HEALTH (CAMH)
1001 Queen Street West, Toronto
www.camh.ca
General inquiries: (416) 595-6111 or 1-800-463-6273 (toll free)

KIDS HELP PHONE
Nationwide, twenty-four-hour, toll-free, confidential crisis line and counselling service available to Canadians under the age of twenty.
org.kidshelpphone.ca/en
1-800-668-6868

MAYO CLINIC
www.mayoclinic.com

NATIONAL SUICIDE PREVENTION LIFELINE
U.S and Canada, twenty-four-hour, toll-free, confidential suicide prevention hotline available to anyone in suicidal crisis or emotional distress.
www.suicidepreventionlifeline.org
1-800-273-TALK (8255)

ONTARIO MINISTRY OF HEALTH
ConnexOntario, mental health and addictions services
www.connexontario.ca
1-519-439-0174

Drug and Alcohol Helpline
www.drugandalcoholhelpline.ca
1-800-565-8603

Mental Health Helpline
www.mentalhealthhelpline.ca
1-866-531-2600

SCHIZOPHRENIA SOCIETY OF ONTARIO
www.schizophrenia.on.ca
1-800-449-6367

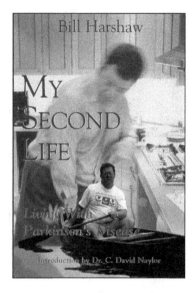

MY SECOND LIFE
Living with Parkinson's Disease
by William A. Harshaw
978-0888822369
$22.99

At the age of thirty-seven, Bill Harshaw was diagnosed with Parkinson's disease. The news changed his life forever, bringing forth a saga that will give hope to not only Parkinsonians, but to people with chronic disease everywhere. *My Second Life* is not a detailed road map or a set of instructions. Instead, it is an account of his changing state of mind over the two decades that he has had Parkinson's disease.

OUT OF THE BLUE
A Memoir of Workplace Depression, Recovery,
Redemption and, Yes, Happiness
by Jan Wong
978-0987868503
$21.99

At the height of her career in journalism, Jan Wong's world came crashing down. A story she wrote about a school shooting sparked a violent backlash, including death threats. Her newspaper failed to stand by her, and for the first time in her life she spiralled into clinical depression. She found herself unable to write, but the paper's management thought she was feigning illness and fired her. Her insurer rejected her claim of depression and her publisher refused to publish this book.

Out of the Blue is a memoir unlike any other. It is the surreal, wrenching, sometimes hilarious, and ultimately triumphant story of one woman's struggle to come to terms with depression.

www.dundurn.com

Visit us at
Dundurn.com | Definingcanada.ca | @dundurnpress | Facebook.com/dundurnpress